~*Praise* for Secrets S...

I highly recommend *Secrets* as an effective and reproducible model of Titus 2 mentoring. Dianne Dougharty is a gifted and extremely creative homemaker and disciple maker. After years of searching for an effective method of mentoring, I believe Dianne has developed a very practical mentoring model. *Secrets* enables "older women" to teach the "younger women" to "love their husbands and children and to be workers at home," thus fulfilling our Biblical mandate. Utilizing a home setting creates an environment that fosters cross-generational friendships and encouragement for the younger women. The combination of discipleship through Biblical devotions and practical home management skills has strengthened our young couples' marriages and thus their families. Their husbands' personal testimonies say it all! I am so grateful for this tool and how it is impacting our church body.

Donna Gaines, pastor's wife, Bellevue Baptist Church

With a perfect blend of practicality and spiritual encouragement, *Secrets* melds the Titus 2 mandate with the need of young women to develop basic homemaking skills. In a culture that often disdains these skills, many young women find themselves unprepared to successfully run their households. And this is when *Secrets* can step into the picture to mentor them! Armed with the leader's guide and student notebook, you will have everything you need to create your own *Secrets* class in your realm of influence. Having used the *Secrets* curriculum in multiple classes in our Women's Ministry over the last three years, I can attest to its effectiveness and impact through the students' heartfelt testimonies. Make a difference in someone's life by teaching her not only the *Secrets* of homemaking but the *Secrets* of life as well.

Marge Lenow, Director of Women's Ministry, Bellevue Baptist Church

From a loving and passionate heart to teach and lead young women to be the wives and mothers God desires women to be, Dianne Dougharty has put into practical form a manual that captures a vision for ministry that is helping young women become the Godly wives and mothers God wants them to be. Having experienced the ministry firsthand by participation for three years with Dianne, I can testify of changed lives and young women excited and grateful for the blessings of the *Secrets Savored* ministry. It not only provides spiritual enrichment and practical application for creating a Godly home, but also wonderful Christian fellowship, new friendships, and lots of fun!

Linda Dawkins, Secrets Savored mentor

Secrets Savored came at the perfect time in my life as a newlywed. With a roomful of new gifts, I was clueless of how to put them all to use without hurting myself in the process! The godly wives that were older and further along in their marriage taught practical tips and gave godly wisdom that provided the proper tools and knowledge to confidently care for my home. The practical aspect of Secrets Savored is perfectly balanced with a biblical lesson that when taught by older, godly women, brings a new outlook for young wives learning how to honor and respect their husbands as an important component to homemaking. One of the many lessons that Secrets Savored taught me is there is more to being a successful housewife than having all the latest kitchen gadgets, a perfectly decorated home, and a gourmet meal prepared. Through Secrets Savored, Dianne Dougharty gave me the godly confidence I needed to embrace the role of being the wife God created and meant me to be for my husband.

Bethany Jerkins, Secrets Savored graduate

Secrets Savored

A Perfect Blend of Practicality and Spiritual Encouragement

• BOOK ONE •

Dianne Dougharty

Leader Guide

SECRETS SAVORED
Book One Leader Guide
Copyright © 2016 by Dianne Lynn Dougharty
All rights reserved.

No part of this publication may be reproduced, stored in a retrieval system, or transmitted
in any form or by any means electronic, mechanical, photocopying, recording,
or otherwise, without the prior written permission of the author.

Scripture quotes are taken from New Living Translation Second Edition, Tyndale House Publishing Company, Carol Stream, Illinois, Copyright ©1968, 1989, 1990, 1991, 1993, 1996, 2004 by Tyndale House Publishing Incorporated. *** Charles Stanley Life Principles Bible Copyright © 2005 by Charles Stanley Holy Bible, New King James Version, Copyright 1982 by Thomas Nelson, Inc.

New American Standard Bible: Ryrie Study Bible, ©1986, 1995 by The Moody Bible Institute.
The New Living Translation Parallel Study Bible, ©2011 by Tyndale House Publishers.
The Message: The Bible in Contemporary Language Copyright © 2002 by Eugene Peterson.
The NIV/Message Parallel Bible Copyright © 2004 The Zondervan Corporation,
Grand Rapids, Michigan 49530.

Library of Congress Control Number: 2012945608
ISBN 978-1533435071

Cover Design & Interior Layout: Amanda Weaver

Printed in the United States of America
U.S. Printing History

First Edition: August 2012

Requests for Information should be addressed to:

Global Ministries Foundation
65 Germantown Court Suite 409
Cordova, Tennessee 38018

Note: For purchasing the Secrets Savored: Book One Leader Guide complete with weekly lesson plans go to www.secretssavored.org. For the Secrets Savored Book One study book go to www.amazon.com.

You will need one workbook per participant.

~To My Life's Partner, Mark Dougharty~

Because of your love, encouragement, sacrifice, and prayers, this ministry exists. Thank you for all the nights you willingly went to bed alone, in order that I could type this material. Thank you for your love, not only for me, but for our Heavenly Father. You have been an incredible example of a man who has given all he is and has to his Savior. You have been so very faithful to me, your family, and the One who gave His life for you. No greater man or prayer warrior exists!

"Therefore, brethren, seek out from among you seven men of good reputation, full of the Holy Spirit and wisdom, whom we may appoint over this business; but we will give ourselves continually to prayer and to the ministry of the word" (Acts 6:3–4, NKJV).

"The Lord our God has secrets known to no one. We are not accountable for them, but we and our children are accountable forever for all that he has revealed to us, so that we may obey all the terms of these instructions."

Deuteronomy 29:29, NLT

"These older women must train the younger women to love their husbands and their children, to live wisely and be pure, to work in their homes, to do good, and to be submissive to their husbands. Then they will not bring shame on the word of God."

Titus 2:4–5, NLT

~Secrets~

By Pat Pope, *Secrets* mentor

Most secrets we share with a friend or two,

But our secrets we share with all of you.

From cooking to cleaning to ironing and such,

We all want to share the secrets so much.

We love to get out a recipe book,

And treat friends and family to something we've cooked.

To keep a neat house is really a must,

So when company arrives, they don't see our dust.

And mending our clothes is a good skill to know,

So you won't find a rip when you're ready to go.

Our homes are our castles, or so it is said,

But that's only true if Christ is the head.

There are no Secrets from Him. He knows when you sin.

To keep your heart clean, on Christ only depend.

We all pray you've learned a small thing or two,

But when questions arise, just call us, PLEASE DO!

~With a Thankful Heart~

I'm afraid if I began to list the names of all those I owe gratitude, I would neglect someone. So, let me begin with the One without whom none of this would be possible, my heavenly Father. I am grateful to the Lord that He knows best. I would have never dreamed that out of life's most difficult hardship, this ministry would be birthed! Thank you, Father!

"The Lord says, 'I will guide you along the best pathway for your life.
I will advise you and watch over you'" (Psalm 32:8, NLT).

I want to thank my church, my pastor, and his wife for their love, encouragement, support, and prayers. Also, for our Women's Ministry director and staff, who were so very patient with this *non-techie* middle-aged woman. To Amanda Weaver, I owe a huge thank you for your service and incredible creativity! Thank you to the Secrets mentors who have faithfully served and blessed my life abundantly; each has been such a joy and encouragement to me. Linda and Marge, thank you for your *editing helps* in making this material the best it could be. To the many young women who participated in the Secrets ministry these past three years, I love you! Thank you for letting us pour into your lives all the *secrets* we have attained over the years. I pray this study and the lives of the leadership have profoundly impacted your life and home.

Thank you, Global Ministries Foundation, for taking us under your ministry wing and believing in what God was doing in and through this ministry. To our board for *t2 Hope for the Home*, thank you for all your tireless work and commitment. To Bart Dahmer, Darya Crockett, Terry Bailey, and all the folks at Innovo Publishing who believed in the value of this material and in the lives of young women, thank you! My heartfelt appreciation goes to the Harry Smith Foundation for the funding to publish this material; you were a direct answer to our prayers!

Thank you to the many folks who have given to Mark and me in so many ways, believed in this ministry, and prayed for us as God has led us down a dark road and through deep waters. There are the *special women* who I must thank for their love, their prayers, their listening ear, the timely hugs, the *"girl!"* moments, the Kleenex supplied, and the laughter, which at times along this journey were much needed and enjoyed—I love you!

Mom, I want to thank you and Dad for your care for me over the years and your sacrifices in parenting me—along with your patience! Also, thank you for your encouragement and belief that I could do anything. I've never doubted your love or support! To my siblings and Mark's family, I am grateful for your love, support, encouragement, prayers, and belief in God's calling upon my life. Last, but certainly not least, I am very grateful to our daughters, our sons-in-law, and grandchildren, for their patience and sacrifice of time away from Mom and Mimi, while I was doing what God had called me to do. How grateful I am for you. You are treasured and loved a bunch!

~Contents~

Weekly Recipes / xi

Book One Schedule / xiv

Introduction to Secrets Savored / xvi

Structure for Secrets Savored Study / xviii

Components of Weekly Session / xx

Week One

Introduction to Secrets Savored: Organizing Your Kitchen /1

Week Two

Back to Basics / 15

Week Three

Kitchen Lingo/27

Week Four

Not Another Trip to the Grocery Store!/45

Week Five

It's 5:30. What's for Dinner?/55

Week Six

Bake a Cake from Scratch? You've Got to Be Kidding! /69

Week Seven

Baking Made Fun and Easy/81

Week Eight

It's a Chinet Evening. Hospitality Made Easy/91

Week Nine

Date Night or Girls Night Out/101

Week Ten

Holiday Ideas: Creative Holiday Decorating and Gift Giving/115

~Weekly Recipes~

Week Two Recipes / 15
Creamy Fruit Dip
Chicken Parmesan
Buttery Beef Stroganoff
Hawaiian Chicken

Week Three Recipes / 27
No-Bake Cookies

Week Four Recipes / 45
Pan Gravy
Thin White Sauce
Slaw Salad with Chicken
Chicken Pizza with Alfredo Sauce
Oriental Chicken Cashew Salad
Tortilla Soup
Chicken Wild Rice Soup
Mile High Potatoes
Kelly's Flank Steak
Honey-Glazed Chicken Breast

Week Five Recipes / 55
Brewed Tea
Grilled Chicken Pasta with Roasted Vegetables and Pesto
Tuscan Salad
Strawberry Trifle
Home-style Pot Roast
Easy Chicken Parmesan
Chicken Wrapped in Bacon
White Bean Chicken Chili
Easy Potato Soup
Quick Vegetable Soup

Week Six Recipes / 69
Cream Cheese Icing
German Chocolate Icing
Seven-Minute Icing
Chocolate Buttercream Icing
Apple and Orange Glaze

Vanilla/Chocolate Frosting
Old-fashioned Sugar Cookies
Mexican Wedding Cookies
Chocolate Fit for a Queen Cupcakes
Checkerboard Cake
Pumpkin Cake Bars
Peanut Butter Swirl Brownies
Pumpkin Bars with Frosting
Cinnamon Chocolate Fudge Brownies
Gooey St. Louis Brownies
Peanut Butter Cookies with a Kiss
Rocky Road Brownies
Raspberry Brownies

Week Seven Recipes / 81
Chocolate Snowflake Cookies
Nancy's Pie Crust
Cathy's Easy Pie Crust
Nancy's Meringue
Chocolate Chess Pie
Cheri's Derby Pie
Walnut Fudge Pie
Best Chess Pie
Mamaw's Coconut Pie
Nancy's Creamy Chocolate Pie
The Best Chocolate Pie
Nancy's Coconut Cream Pie
Hot Apple Pie
Summer Quiche
Cathy's Easy Quiche
Quick Baking Mix/Recipes
Quick Bread Recipes
Yeast Bread Recipes

Week Eight Recipes / 91
Sausage Vegetable Soup
Bibb Salad with Raspberry Dressing
Formal Menu: Phyllo Cheese Tarts
Grilled Beef Tenderloin with Mushroom Sauce
Mashed Red Potatoes
Vegetable-Stuffed Tomatoes
Chocolate Hazelnut Torte

Casual Menu: Black-eyed Pea Salsa
Chicken Tortilla Soup
Chocolate Chip Cookies
Homemade Buttery Pecan Ice Cream

Week Nine Recipes / 101

Girls Flannel Night Recipe: Buttery Sweet Popcorn
Girls Bake Night Recipe: Peanut Butter Milk Chocolate Crescents

Week Ten Recipes / 115

Fall Recipes: Apple and Spice Sugar Glazed Turkey
Baked Sweet Mashed Potatoes
Make Ahead Turkey Gravy
Brussels Sprouts with Apples
Green Beans with Roquefort Cheese and Walnuts
Cornbread Stuffing
Chestnut Chocolate Tassies
Perfect Pecan Pie
Christmas Recipes: Creamy Caramel Sauce
Eggnog Coffee Punch
Crescent Pesto Appetizers
Cheddar and Tomato Spread
Barbecue Meatballs
Chocolate Peppermint Parfaits
Nutty Cinnamon Palmiers
Praline Coffee
Mary's Christmas Morning Orange Julius

~Book One Schedule~

Week One: *Introduction to Secrets: Organizing Your Kitchen.* Introduce the young women to the Secrets study and the benefits of having an organized kitchen. The *Krazy Kitchen Trivia* or the *Whatcha Know* sheet can be used as an activity in order to see how knowledgeable the young women are about the kitchen and homemaking.

Week Two: *Back to Basics.* Play *The Gadget Game*; identify the necessary utensils needed for working in the kitchen and their usage. Teach on using substitutions in cooking. Cover basic pantry needs, discussing the necessity of each item.

Week Three: *Kitchen Lingo.* Play a game of *Kitchen Lingo Bingo* to teach terms used in cooking. Define and demonstrate several terms often used in recipes. Explain the importance of proper measuring in cooking. Discuss the weights and measurement chart and prepare a recipe of *No-Bake Cookies* to illustrate measuring dry versus wet ingredients.

Week Four: *Not Another Trip to the Grocery Store!* Teach meal planning and effective grocery store shopping; couponing can be included. Prepare one of the recipes for a quick and easy meal using a roasted chicken. Demonstrate how to make gravy and the white sauce called for in the chicken pizza recipe. Recipes are included in this week's lesson for using a roasted chicken to serve two additional *Easy Recipes*.

Week Five: *It's 5:30, What's for Dinner?* Play the *Spice It Up* game. Give tips on freezing and discuss freezing foods in relationship to preparing easy meals. Discuss spices and their necessity in cooking. Prepare the easy meal recipe given in the lesson and demonstrate the process for making brewed tea.

Week Six: *Bake a Cake from Scratch? You've Got to Be Kidding!* Play the *Matchin' and Bakin' Game* to introduce baking terms. Have a variety of baking utensils on display; describe the utensils and their usage. Show a variety of bakeware. Using handouts, explain baking pan substitutions. Using one of the icing recipes, demonstrate how to ice a cake or select another baking activity found in this week's lesson.

Week Seven: *Baking Made Fun and Easy.* Review the importance of proper measurements, especially in baking. Show a variety of measuring utensils for baking and explain their proper usage. Provide chilled dough for making the *Snowflake Cookies* or select another baking activity provided in this week's lesson, such as making a piecrust with filling. Have a few *Quick Breads* on hand for the girls to taste at *Snack Time*.

Week Eight: *It's a Chinet Evening: Hospitality Made Easy.* Discuss the importance of hospitality, and the *how-to* of hosting guests in one's home. Teach proper place settings. Cover the appropriate rules of serving. Prepare a meal idea found in the *Hospitality Made Fun and Affordable* section.

Week Nine: *Date Night.* For young married women, host a dinner in the hostess's home. Leadership and spouses prepare and serve dinner to the young women and their husbands. Use *Creative Questions and Conversation Starters* in Week Four for questions to be placed at each table for promoting conversation. For college/single young women, have a *Girls' Night Out*. (See Week Nine Lesson Plan for suggestions.)

Week Ten: *A Thanksgiving and Christmas to Remember—Creative Holiday Decorating and Gift Giving.* The participants in the class are encouraged to invite friends to share in this special class. A variety of guests are invited to demonstrate creative holiday ideas for the home, including creative gifts to make for friends and family, as well as, decorations for the home, *all on an affordable budget!* The leadership will provide samplings of their favorite holiday recipes. Hostess provides drinks and coffee.

~Introduction to Secrets Savored~

In today's culture, we have eliminated Home Economics from our educational system. Due to this and other contributing factors, we are seeing a generation of young women unprepared to be wives, moms, and homemakers. Many have grown up in a single-parent home, mostly due to the increased number of divorces. They lacked role models and have grown up in a society where being a homemaker receives no honorable recognition. Quite often, the young women of today are overwhelmed with the responsibility of caring for home and family; they are frustrated and feel unfulfilled.

Dennis Rainey of *Family Life Today* related a story in a recent newsletter that fully illustrates what I am trying to convey about this current generation:

> In a recent staff meeting, Bill Eyster, the chief operating officer of Family Life, shared a story I just can't get out of my mind. His daughter—a high school senior this year in a Christian school—was studying marriage and the book of Ephesians in her Bible class. The teacher asked, "How many of you want a marriage like your parents?" Now for the shocker . . . out of the 25 kids in class, only two raised their hands. Less than 10 percent! And this was a Christian school. Stunning! I know it's an informal survey, but if we use that classroom as a standard, it means that 90 percent of this generation DO NOT see their parents' marriage as something to emulate. Many are not being raised in "homes," but in "houses"—meaningless structures often void of authentic relationships, trust, spiritual encouragement, and togetherness. They are aimless and morally vulnerable, preyed upon by evil. It is a generation at risk for living out a self-perpetual scenario. They may live in a great house, but in truth, they are **HOMELESS** just as surely as someone who sleeps in the street. What I believe this "Homeless Generation" is yearning for, and not seeing in their families, are healthy relationships built on love, commitment, forgiveness, selflessness, and underlying peace that weathers any storm. They are the least parented generation ever. What will they use as their blueprints to build their own homes in the future?

There are two sources for the *blueprint* that is needed for this "homeless generation." The first is God's Word. The older women know the truths that lie within His Word and are to teach those truths to the younger women. The second source is the lives of *experienced, seasoned* women, those who have learned much throughout their years as wives, moms, and homemakers. It is *our* responsibility to teach this current generation.

For several years now, I have desired to find a way to teach young women how to be effective homemakers and to value their God-given calling. Many have expressed to me an interest in being *discipled* in the area of homemaking. Thus, the *Secrets Savored* material was birthed in order to meet this critical need.

When God began to open a door to offer this study, I was searching for a name. One afternoon, I was in my kitchen and noticed a book on the shelf entitled *Secrets*; I had ordered the book from *Southern Living*. The book contained all the results of the tests done in the *Southern Living* test kitchens. I thought, *What woman doesn't like to know a secret?* Deuteronomy 29:29 NLT says, *"The Lord our God has secrets known to no one. We are not accountable for them, but we and our children are accountable forever for all that he has revealed to us, so that we may obey all the terms of these instructions."* Then I turned to Titus 2:4–5 NLT, which says that older women are to teach and encourage the younger women to *"love their husbands, and their children, to live wisely and be pure, to work in their homes, to do good, and to be submissive to their husbands. Then they will not bring shame on the word of God."* As older, experienced women, we have acquired an abundance of "secrets" throughout the years. It is our responsibility to share the many things we have learned with this generation of young women. It is also our responsibility to teach them the *secrets* and *treasures* found within God's Word. The verse in Deuteronomy says there are some things God chooses to keep to Himself, but what He has revealed to us, His children, is our responsibility to teach others. This study is designed so that we as older, experienced women can fulfill the mandate given to us in Titus 2. My desire is that the *secrets* you and I have learned throughout the years will be of help practically and spiritually in the lives of younger women.

In the pages to follow, you will find a study structured for a group of ten to twelve young women led by a leadership team of three to four experienced (older) women. In these pages, and through the lives of the Secret's leadership, the young women will learn the secret and joy of fulfilling the role of homemaker, wife, and mom.

The *Secrets Savored* study is from the Father, and He has given the material in the following pages. To Him be all glory, honor, and praise!

Dianne
Titus 2:4–5

~Structure for Secrets Savored Study~

- **Secrets Savored** encompasses two exciting books designed to meet the needs of young women. **Book One** provides eight weeks of lessons all related to the kitchen, with a variety of topics such as: organizing your kitchen, cooking, baking, meal planning and hospitality. **Book Two** is a nine week continuation of practical instruction on caring for the home, with a variety of topics such as: organizing your home, shopping your closet, etiquette and gardening. Time allotted for each class should be 2½- 3 hours per session.

- The cost for each course should be determined by the organization offering **Secrets Savored**. A fee of $25-$30 per session is recommended and should cover the expense of the **Book One Study Book**, supplies purchased by the leadership for the baking/cooking activities each week, and Door Prizes (optional). Note: For purchasing the **Secrets Savored: Book One Leader Guide** complete with weekly lesson plans or the study book go to www.secretssavored.org

- A leadership team of three to four is recommended for each Secrets Savored class of 10-12 young women. You will need one woman to serve as the teaching leader, one or two assistant leaders and a home hostess.

Secrets Leadership Responsibilities:

Leader: Each week, the leader will have the overall responsibility of teaching the Practical Lesson and providing all the materials and supplies needed, with the help of the home hostess and other leadership. She will make contacts outside of class with the students as necessary.

Assistant Leaders/Mentors: These women will fill in for the leader when necessary and will contribute to each of the lessons as determined at the weekly meeting prior to the upcoming class. Assistants/Mentors will be called upon to give input, especially in the areas where they are knowledgeable and to help in teaching the devotional lesson each week (optional for those who are not comfortable). As needed, the assistants will share the responsibility of contacting the young women outside of class. For Example: If a young woman were absent, a phone call or text would be made or a note written.

Home Hostess: The home hostess is a part of the leadership team. She should be willing to provide coffee/beverages and some supplies from her kitchen as needed for the Practical Lessons.

Team Meeting: It is recommended that the team meet once a week prior to class- via email or text may be necessary due to other commitments. An option for a day time class would be to meet over lunch following the Secrets Savored class; this is a good time to plan for the coming week's lesson and divide responsibilities.

The Leader Guide, available on-line at www.secretssavored.org, is complete with a Weekly Introduction, Practical Lesson Plan, an Equipment List (necessary for kitchen activities) and a Weekly Devotional Lesson.

The **Study Notebook** includes a Weekly Introduction, Weekly Lesson Sheets and a Weekly Devotional Lesson Sheet.

Secrets Savored Curriculum:

- **Book One of Secrets Savored** provides eight weeks of lessons filled with recipes, and practical instruction related to the kitchen, cooking, baking, meal planning and hospitality.

- **Book Two of Secrets Savored** provides nine weeks of lessons filled with additional recipes, and practical instruction on caring for a home, laundry/ironing, proper etiquette (for adults and children), shopping your closet, hospitality and the art of gardening.

- The **Bible Study** in **Books One** and **Two** takes an up-close look at the women of the Bible. Each week we study the biblical principles found in their life stories and apply it to the lives of the women participating in the study.

- **Secrets Savored Books Three and Four- Life's Moments Made Simple** were written due to the desire of young women for a follow-up study to **Secrets Savored**. This study includes additional practical instruction, along with an in-depth Bible study. As women maneuver through life, they face many issues, such as contentment, fear, anxiety, worry, difficult relationships etc. In this study, the young women look into God's Word for Biblical principles concerning these issues. Those principles, when applied, strengthen their walk with Christ and enable them to live purposefully and victoriously. In addition to the Bible study, there are unique practical tools for helping simplify their daily lives through receiving weekly meal plans, a variety of great recipes, short-cuts for meal preparation and tips on healthy eating.

~Components of Weekly Session~

Devotional Lesson—Each week's lesson is a study of a woman in the *Bible* and is designed to be 20-30 minutes in length. Practical and Biblical life lessons are taken from the lives of the women studied and then applied to the lives of those participating in the study. The weekly teaching time may vary based on the topic. The devotional is located in the back of each week's lesson in the *Leader Guide*.

Practical Lesson—Each week's lesson will cover 1½- 2 hours. If the lesson calls for **Time in the Kitchen,** students will be participating in an instructional activity in the kitchen. This activity is given to support and illustrate the practical lesson being taught. Each week is filled with teaching topics and suggestions–the leadership will determine according to the time allotted which of the suggested topics and activities can be accomplished. Note: The **Book Two** curriculum on the home provides activities that include some cooking and baking, an ironing demonstration, a cleaning demonstration, preparing homemade laundry detergent and cleaners, painting techniques etc. **Book Two** will have limited **Time in the Kitchen** due to the subject matter covered.

Weekly Lesson Sheets—This is a list of the Lesson Sheets included in the **Leader Guide**.

Equipment List—This is a detailed list of all the items and equipment required for each week's lesson. The responsibility for these should be divided among the leadership.

Door Prizes—Door prizes are optional. The items purchased should be inexpensive and relate to the subject taught. They can either be donated by leadership or a portion of the monies collected for the class can be set aside to purchase these. The process for giving out Door Prizes will be determined by the leadership.

Helpful Hints—The Helpful Hints sheets are found in several chapters and are filled with tips for making life easier as the young women maneuver their way through the homemaking process.

Snack Time—Leadership will provide a snack each week and the home hostess will provide the drinks. If offering an evening class, many young women come from work and have not had dinner, so make sure the snack is substantial. Note: On the weeks food is prepared, no snack is necessary.

~ Instructions for Bible Study ~

The main purpose in studying God's Word is so that we will know Him. If we know the Bible we will thus know the God of the Bible.

Psalm 119:11 says, "I have hidden your word in my heart that I might not sin against you."(NIV) God's Word informs, instructs, guides, corrects and convicts us. It is life and breath to us as Christians. If we *hide* it in our hearts we will always have a word of encouragement and instruction to draw upon.

Our purpose in studying women of the Bible is because we believe it was no mistake that God placed women within His story. Women are relational, and women relate to other women; God made us that way.

There are Biblical principles that we can glean from each one. In studying Sarah, Abraham's wife, we learn about the Biblical principle of *waiting on God* and the consequences of not waiting on Him. And from Rahab we learn the Biblical principle of *obedience equals blessing*. Her faith led her to trust that God would take care of her and her family. She obeyed the spy's instructions and was saved along with her family. God blessed her by placing her in the lineage of Christ. She is mentioned in Hebrews Chapter 11, the Faith Hall of Fame.

Many of the women we will be studying over the next few weeks made good choices, but then, others made bad choices. In life, we all make some good and some bad choices. In studying these women, we will see the blessings of good choices and the consequences of bad choices. God has placed each one within His story so that you and I might learn from their lives.

Leadership Responsibility—The responsibility of the leadership team is to teach the devotional each week.

Teaching Time—Each lesson should not exceed 20-30 minutes and has ample material for the time allotted. The mentor who is teaching has the discretionary freedom to use as much or as little of the material, as they deem necessary.

Biblical History Section—This section is placed within the lesson for the purpose of giving the teaching mentor Biblical background and information. It is not to be read aloud, strictly a resource.

Questions to Ponder—These questions are not included in each week's lesson. When they are, they can be found at the end of the week's question section. These are given for the class participants to pray over and ponder as to the application in their own lives.

Dianne's Personal Testimony—This section is placed within the lesson in order to share personal life experiences related to today's lesson. The leadership may have personal testimonies that would fit within.

Week 1

Introduction to
Secrets Savored
Organizing your Kitchen

Week One: Introduction to Secrets Savored / Organizing Your Kitchen

Week One Lesson Plan

I. Getting to Know You

- Greet each young woman upon arrival. Hand out books, name tags, and collect class fee. Have each participant turn to page 5 the Getting to Know You sheet. Ask them to mingle, filling in the sheet as instructed at the top. Once everyone has arrived, and had time to mingle, be seated and using the activity sheet discuss the contents of the sheet as a means of getting acquainted.

II. Devotional

- The devotionals to be studied each week will begin in Week Two and continue through Week Eight.

III. Leader Opens in Prayer

- Introduce the Secrets study and explain objective for the ministry. Give an overview of the coming semester. Allow time for answering questions.

- Introduce the leadership team.

- Divide the young women into groups of two to three. Choose one of the activity sheets offered: Whatcha Know or Krazy Kitchen Trivia.

- Allow the young women ten minutes to work as a team and complete their sheets. Discuss the answers. The team with the greatest number correct will receive prizes.

- Move to the kitchen.

IV. Time in the Kitchen

- In introducing the young women to the kitchen, explain that just as the *hub* is the center of activity in an airport, the kitchen is the *hub* of a home. A great deal takes place in the kitchen. Because this is true, things will run much smoother if it is organized. Can you imagine an unorganized airport? What chaos there would be! Discuss the importance of having an organized kitchen—what it looks like and why certain items belong in specific places. *For Example:* The drinking glasses should be near the refrigerator, and the silverware and dinnerware should be close to the table and dishwasher.

- Demonstrate an organized drawer versus an unorganized drawer and how to get the maximum use of limited space. *For Example*: Kitchen towels and dishrags can be neatly rolled in order to get the maximum number into a small drawer. Show examples of cost friendly and practical equipment sold at your local hardware or other stores to help get the kitchen organized and running more efficiently. Leadership may want to share items from their own kitchen that have helped them to have a more organized kitchen.

- Suggest ways to organize recipes. *For Example*: Place recipes in files on your computer categorized by: Entrées, Salads, Soups and Breads, Vegetables, Desserts. When using a photo album to store recipes, label each album by category in order to keep recipes organized and easily accessible.

- Refer to the *Food Safety* sheet. Explain the dangers of *E coli* in dealing with raw meats and the importance of antibacterial cleaners in the kitchen.

- Leadership will provide a weekly snack and beverage. Use this time to get to know the young women and answer questions about today's lesson.

- Have each participant fill out the Secrets Savored Participant Info Sheet before leaving class.

V. Week One Lesson Sheets

    INTRODUCTION: A Heart Set on Learning
    SECRETS SAVORED PARTICIPATION INFO SHEET
    GETTING TO KNOW YOU
    WHATCHA KNOW ACTIVITY SHEET
    WHATCHA KNOW ANSWER SHEET
    KRAZY KITCHEN TRIVIA ACTIVITY SHEET
    KRAZY KITCHEN TRIVIA ANSWER SHEET
    TEACHING NOTES: GETTING YOUR KITCHEN ORGANIZED

VI. Equipment for Week One

- Name tags and pens

- Kitchen drawers: one messy and one organized

- Organizing equipment: Rubbermaid organizational trays and containers, spice stand, lazy Susan, trays, and caddies—items that would keep a kitchen organized and neat

- Provide items and ideas for organizing recipes. *For Example:* A recipe box, photo album, and an example of an online system

- Demonstrate how to make sure your kitchen counters are safe after opening a package of raw meat, using Clorox® wipes or other disinfectants to clean space

- Door prizes/Prizes for winners of activity sheet

Introduction: A Heart Set on Learning

In the summer of 1969, between my seventh- and eighth-grade year, my family moved back to Nashville, Tennessee, where we had lived prior to my parents attending the University of Kansas. Beginning a new school and making friends at that age was quite a challenge; let's just say it was the pits! I was looking for ways to meet the girls in my grade, so when I had a chance to sign up for Home Economics, an all-girls class, I took it. This particular class is probably not familiar to today's young women, but yes, they did actually offer a class where young women could discover the foundations of keeping a home. In Home Economics, students worked together to learn how to bake, cook, and do basic sewing.

Our teacher also taught proper etiquette. We seldom hear those words today. *Etiquette* is "the prescribed rules, form and practices, established for behavior in polite society or in official or professional life." Now you know! It was easy for me to make friends in my home economics class. I really enjoyed going each day. It was a nice change from English, math, history, and the rest of my schedule.

As a part of our overall grade, we were expected to eat what we had prepared. I will never forget the day we cooked fried okra. Okay, it is finally time for me to confess. I found the pockets in my apron—yes, we were required to wear an apron!—quite handy that day for dispensing my fried okra from my plate to the corner trash can. To this day, I have absolutely no desire to have fried okra.

Secrets Savored is not a school course; there will be no tests or final exams. You will not be forced to eat what you cook. We, as leaders, are not trained or certified teachers, just women who have, through the years, acquired wisdom, knowledge, skills, and numerous "secrets" in the area of being a wife, mom, and homemaker.

In the weeks to follow, there will be some subjects concerning homemaking you will love and others you will not like at all. That's okay! I love to iron, but I really dislike vacuuming; however, there are times when I have to do both. The vacuuming occurs *only* when my husband is not there to do it for me!

We, the leadership, would ask only three things of you: 1) to faithfully attend each week, 2) to participate in the activities, and 3) that you would have *a heart set on learning*. This study is designed to be fun, informative, and educational. You will be drawn to the subjects you love and for those you do not like, you will probably do anyway, out of necessity. Such is the life of a homemaker!

Secrets Savored Participation Info Sheet

Name:

Married: 1–5 years____ 6–10 years____ More than 10 years____

Age: 15–22____ 23–30____ 31–35____ over 35____

E-Mail Address:

Home Address:

Home Phone#:

Cell Phone#:

Allergies:

Tell us about yourself: (Example: Where did you go to school? Where do you work? Where did you grow up? Do you have any unusual life experiences? Do you have any children? If so, how many and what are their ages?)

Getting to Know You

Find one girl with whom you have each of the following statements in common and have her initial that statement.

Find someone who is wearing the same color top.

Find someone who has lived in the city the same number of years as you have.

Find someone with the same color eyes.

Find someone whose favorite hobby is the same as yours.

Find someone who has the same number of siblings.

Find someone who has three of the same digits in their cell phone number.

Find someone who has at least two of the same letters in their last name as you.

Find someone who shares your birth month or year.

Whatcha Know Activity Sheet

True or False:

1. Decaffeinated coffee is made from coffee beans that have been soaked or steamed to allow all the caffeine to diffuse from the beans. In the process, 97 percent of the caffeine is removed.

2. Cinnamon sticks can be grated with a grater that has small holes and then used as ground cinnamon.

3. There is no difference between chopping, mincing, cubing, and dicing in cooking.

4. A frittata is an Italian sandwich that resembles a crustless quiche.

5. Frosting is the same as icing.

6. There is a difference between French bread and Italian bread.

7. Rosemary, cilantro, tarragon, and thyme are among some of the strongest herbs.

8. Dark and light molasses are interchangeable in cooking.

9. To prevent sliced peaches from browning, sprinkle with lemon juice and toss lightly.

10. A truffle is a layered English dessert usually served in a glass dish.

11. The time a turkey cooks is based on the weight of the turkey.

12. Bleached flour is wheat flour that has been treated with a whitening agent and can be used interchangeably with all-purpose flour.

13. If a recipe calls for buttermilk and you do not have any, there is no substitute, and you are out of luck!

14. Three medium apples are equal to 1½ cups of chopped apples.

15. One half cup of Splenda is equal to one half cup of granulated sugar.

16. Fondant is a French word referring to a food that is cooked at the table in a ceramic lined metal bowl.

Whatcha Know Answer Sheet

1. True

2. True

3. False. *Chopping* is cutting food into irregular pieces about the size of a pea. *Mincing* is chopping food into tiny irregular pieces. *Cubing* is cutting food into uniform pieces of the same size, usually about ½ inch on each side. *Dicing* is similar to cubing, except the pieces are ⅛ to ¼ inch on each side.

4. False: an Italian omelet.

5. True

6. True: French bread loaves are usually a bit longer, narrower, and have a crisper crust than the Italian bread loaves.

7. True: You can also add oregano and sage to this list; use sparingly. Medium-flavored herbs are basil, dill, mint, and fennel. Delicate herbs like parsley and chive can be used generously.

8. True: The dark molasses is usually not as sweet as the light and the foods prepared with the dark take on a darker color.

9. True: Orange juice can be used as well in preventing peaches from turning brown as well as any carbonated citrus drink. *For Example*: Sprite or 7-Up.

10. False: *Truffle*: French chocolate candy. *Trifle*: an English dessert.

11. True

12. True

13. False: Use 1 tablespoon lemon juice or vinegar plus whole milk to make 1 cup. Let stand ten minutes.

14. True

15. True

16. False: *Fondue* is a French word referring to food cooked at the table.

Krazy Kitchen Trivia Activity Sheet

1. This cookie debuted in 1912 and since then, 362 billion have been sold; it is considered the best-selling cookie in the United States.

2. What company did the name Nabisco originate from?

3. In 1853, George Crum was the chef at an elegant resort in Saratoga, New York. He was the creator of a snack food now consumed by millions. In 1860, he opened his first restaurant featuring these snacks in baskets on every table.

4. This food item is second in human consumption only to rice.

5. In 1932, a company was started in Nashville and is now the largest seller of an American salty snack food.

6. Turbinado and muscovado are names of what type of food?

7. This kitchen instrument has a broad, flat, flexible blade used to mix, spread, and lift in cooking or baking. The term for this instrument originated in England in 1525.

8. This kitchen appliance was invented in 1908 by Herbert Johnson, an engineer for the Hobart Manufacturing Company. In 1919, Mr. Johnson started his own company manufacturing his eighty-quart machine that would be used in bakeries all over the world.

9. It takes twenty-one pounds of fresh, wholesome cow's milk to make one pound of this creamy dairy product.

10. In early times, this kitchen cookware stood on three legs, which allowed it to be positioned over an open fire.

11. This food product was mentioned often in the Bible and has been around for hundreds of years. It is often enjoyed with a meal.

12. The jingle from this cleaning product ad was the longest running jingle on American television and was sung by Don Cherry and Betty Bryan. This cleaner was the first liquid cleaner to be sold in a plastic bottle.

13. This cleaning product was introduced in 1958 and was the first such product to be released in a spray form.

14. Prior to 1797, these cleaning tools were handmade using grass, hay, straw, fine twigs, and corn husks.

15. This screw-neck bottle was patented by John Mason.

16. German engineer Carl von Linde patented the first process of liquefying gas in 1876, which is the basic technology of this kitchen appliance.

17. In 1801, Josiah Bent Bakery in Milton, Massachusetts, created this bakery product that has accompanied a bowl of soup for years.

18. This basic pantry product appears in 97 percent of American homes. The first recipe was printed in Elizabeth Smith's *The Complete Housewife* in 1727. It called for anchovies, shallots, vinegar, white wine, sweet spices, pepper, and lemon peel. More recent recipes call for tomato, vinegar, sugar, salt, allspice, cloves, and cinnamon. It is considered a moderate health benefit, as it contains lycopene.

Krazy Kitchen Trivia Answer Sheet

1. OREOS

2. NATIONAL BISCUIT COMPANY

3. THE POTATO CHIP

4. POTATOES

5. LAYS POTATO CHIP COMPANY

6. NATURAL BROWN SUGAR

7. THE SPATULA

8. ELECTRIC STAND MIXER—KITCHEN AID

9. BUTTER

10. THE CAST IRON SKILLET

11. LOAF OF BREAD

12. MR. CLEAN

13. PLEDGE

14. THE BROOM

15. MASON JAR

16. THE REFRIGERATOR

17. THE SALTINE CRACKER

18. KETCHUP

Teaching Notes: Getting Your Kitchen Organized[1]

Questions to ask when organizing your kitchen:

1. Are the things you use every day stored where you can easily get to them?

2. How high can you comfortably reach?

3. Are you right or left handed? Short or tall? Do you or any other family members have any physical limitations? How might you rearrange countertops and storage spaces to accommodate your family's needs? (This could be as simple as moving the dish drainer to the opposite side of the sink.)

4. Are spices stored near the stove and organized for easy access?

5. Are items stored in places that make sense so guests can easily find what they need?

6. Can you reach cooking utensils without moving from the stove?

7. Are napkins, dinnerware, placemats, and salt and pepper shakers handy to the dinner table?

When organizing your kitchen, keep the following in mind:

1. Store items where they are most often used. Instead of asking, "Where can I store this?" ask yourself, "Where do I use this?" Strive for one-motion storage. *For Example*: the coffeemaker should be close to the sink or water dispenser. Coffee and filters should be within arm's reach.

2. Create work centers. Envision your kitchen in terms of the tasks you perform there (chopping, baking, lunch making, and so forth). Arrange accordingly. Try to revolve each center around an appliance, some storage space, and a workspace. Store equipment and food near the work center where they'll be used.

3. Give *daily used* items space priority. Don't keep your Bundt pan, which you use infrequently, in front of saucepans you use daily.

4. Give every item a home. Whenever you acquire a new item, be it a pitcher or pasta maker, choose a storage spot as soon as you bring it home. For bigger items, it is a good idea to figure this out beforehand.

5. Store things in smart ways. Place glassware and cups upside down to prevent dust and discourage insects. Store rice, beans, cornmeal, flour, and dry staples in sealed, see-through containers. You'll keep pests at bay and always know supply levels.

6. Keep only what you use. Say goodbye to space-taking cookbooks you haven't opened in years. Cut out your favorite recipes and file them in an album. Donate the punch bowl!

7. Make a wish list. Write a list of kitchen items you'd like to buy as your budget allows. Keep it handy so when your favorite local kitchen store has a sale or your sister asks what you want for your birthday, you're ready.

---

[2] Kathy Peel, "Is Your Kitchen User-Friendly," *HomeLife*, no.1 (March 2011):52–53.

Back to Basics

Week 2

Week Two: Back to Basics

Week Two Lesson Plan

I. Leader opens in prayer.

II. Devotional

- *Eve—A Woman of Influence.* Read Genesis 1:26, 2:7–9, 15–25, and 3:1–16. (For help in preparing, refer to lesson outline in Devotional section of Leader Guide.)

III. Lesson

- Play The Gadget Game. Place a variety of ten utensils on the dining or kitchen table and label with numbered stickers. Using The Gadget Game sheet, have the young women look at each utensil, and without discussion, fill in the blanks on their sheet with the appropriate name of each utensil.

- Once sheets are completed, check to see if they can name each and explain its use. Referring to the Basic Kitchen Utensils sheet, discuss any utensils listed that the young woman are unfamiliar with, showing examples of each if possible.

IV. Time in the Kitchen

- Discuss substitutions in cooking; refer to the Cooking and Baking Substitutions sheet. Choose an easy recipe of your own to demonstrate the use of substitutions in cooking or prepare one recipe of the Creamy Fruit Dip. For Dip: Cut the recipe in half using sour cream in one half and the substitute of yogurt in the other half. Serve with sliced apples and graham cracker sticks. Compare the flavors of the two recipes.

- For demonstrating utensil usage while you are teaching substitutions, have two to four of the young women use a corer to core the apples, a peeler to peel the apples, and a paring knife to slice the apples. Demonstrate how to use these utensils. For additional demonstration, use a whisk to mix the dip.

- If time allows, demonstrate how to make a buttermilk substitute. Take 1 cup of room temperature milk and add 2 T. vinegar or 2 T. lemon juice. Let stand for 10 minutes and you will have a buttermilk substitute for your Saturday morning pancakes! (Refer to the Cooking and Baking Substitutions chart in the Student Notebook.)

- Go over the Basic Pantry Needs for Your Kitchen.

- Read one of the following scenarios to illustrate the purpose of having a well-stocked pantry. *Married Young Women:* Scenario #1: It is 4:30 p.m. and your son has been running a fever all day. You have not been able to go the grocery store in order to get groceries for dinner. What do you have on hand in the pantry that would allow you to prepare a meal by six o'clock, when your husband arrives home?

Single Young Women: Scenario #2: *You have been working twelve-hour days for a solid week, your parents are coming into town this evening, and you will just have enough time to run by the store quickly to get a meat item and then home to get a meal on, barely making it to the airport before their plane lands. What are you going to prepare that would be edible?* Leadership, taking some of the items from the *Basic Pantry Needs* list (both pantry and refrigerator items), give the young women one or two meal ideas they could prepare in each situation. (Three recipes are given in the Leader Guide and Student Notebook that can be prepared with the items on the basic pantry items list, adding an additional one to three items purchased at the local grocery.)

- Answer questions. Give out prizes.

V. Week Two Lesson Sheets

    INTRODUCTION: A Knife and a Shoe
    THE GADGET GAME
    DEVOTIONAL: Eve

VI. Equipment for Week Two

- Ten utensils for *The Gadget Game* and a variety of utensils to show and demonstrate their usage

- Provide samples of items found on the pantry list. Be sure to have on hand the ingredients to demonstrate being able to prepare a meal at the last minute with basic pantry items

- Apples and graham crackers for the Creamy Fruit Dip—all ingredients to make one recipe including sour cream and yogurt. Apple corer, apple peeler, and paring knife to be used by girls to prepare apples for tasting dip. The leadership may want to show the usage of a whisk or other utensil in preparing the dip. Have the container of sour cream and the container of yogurt used in preparing the recipe for demonstration

- One-cup capacity glass measuring cup filled with room temperature milk. Two tablespoons vinegar or lemon

- Plates and napkins for tasting dip

- Prizes for *The Gadget Game*

Introduction: A Knife and a Shoe

Have you ever tried to peel a potato with a knife? If you have, you know that typically you end up losing half of the potato! Have you ever tried to drive a nail into a wall with a shoe instead of a hammer? It doesn't work very well, does it? Using the proper utensils or tools makes the job you are doing much easier. Homemaking is much easier if we have the proper *equipment* and if we are able to find them. Where was that hammer, anyway? It should have been in the catchall drawer, along with the peeler, the rubber bands, the children's schoolwork, the pens, etc. You know that drawer, don't you? Everyone has one of those drawers, right? Maybe the proper name would be the junk drawer.

I grew up in a home with a very creative and frugal dad. We had very little money, so he was always looking for ways to fix things with the supplies that were available in our home. Sometimes it worked and sometimes it didn't. One time, he worked on a faucet in the kitchen; we are not sure exactly what he did or what tools he used. We do know that after he finished, the hot-water side was cold, the cold-water side was hot, and it took a sledgehammer to raise the handle! We just laughed and figured eventually the handle would loosen and over time we would get used to the hot being cold and the cold being hot!

Having the right *equipment* and being able to find it is very important. Over the years, I have discovered that some people are naturally organized and others are not. My dad grew up in a home with twelve siblings during the Depression. He never threw anything away; on the other hand, my mom likes things neat and organized. I take after my mom. I was born with a mind that *thinks organization*. When Mark and I go out to run errands, I have laid out in my mind the most efficient route before we ever leave the house. His mind does not work that way at all, and for that, he is grateful. Because his mind does not work that way, he escapes the responsibility of loading the car every time we head out on a trip. He has said numerous times, "There's no way all that stuff is going into that trunk." Somehow, it all gets in! Like they say, "Where there's a will and an organized mind, there's a way."

Having a work area *organized* helps us to be more efficient. Your kitchen is a work area. Sure, you have fun there and, yes, you make memories there, but the main activity of a kitchen is work. So, if your hammer and your peeler are buried in the *junk* drawer and you have to use a knife and a shoe, the work will not get done as efficiently.

The Gadget Game

1. _____

2. _____

3. _____

4. _____

5. _____

6. _____

7. _____

8. _____

9. _____

10. _____

WEEK TWO: Eve—A Woman of Influence

Read Genesis 1:26, NASB: "*Let us make man in our image, according to our likeness; and let them rule over the fish of the sea and over the birds of the sky and over the cattle and over all the earth, and over every creeping thing that creeps on the earth. God created man in His own image, in the image of God He created him; male and female He created them.*"

Read Genesis 2:7–9, 15–25, 3:1–16

In these verses we see:

- God is the Creator of all the earth and everything on the earth.
- He created man.
- Man was put on the earth as God's representative, created in the image of God.
- God had two desires in creating woman. First, in order that man would not be alone—to give him a helpmate. Second, for multiplication.

In the book entitled *The New Eve* by Robert Lewis,[2] he refers to various women throughout history as "history turners." Speaking of Eve, he says, "History is full of women who have reshaped our world in one way or another. But, no woman has turned history so significantly or as permanently as the first woman: Eve."

Lewis goes on to say, "Satan's deception of Eve brought us to a cataclysmic moment that today still affects us all. Most of us know it simply as the FALL. It was a moment when all God's original intentions and core callings for you as a woman (and really all mankind) became twisted, distorted, and, most of all, DIFFICULT."

Let's take a look at what happened to Eve. We see her in the garden. It was the perfect place, a beautiful place, and within it, Eve had all she needed.

Adam and Eve had a visitor in the garden—not the kind of company you or I would like to have for a visit. Satan was there disguised as a serpent. He blended right into the garden. Occasionally, snakes are found in a garden, and quite often we hear their hissing before we actually see them.

Dianne: *Several years ago, I was watering a hanging basket in the back yard and as the water hit the soil, I heard hissing. I dropped the bucket and ran. The snake had wound itself within the basket, blending right in with the plant.*

As he approaches her, he says, "*Indeed has God said, you shall not eat from any tree of the garden?*" What he desires of Eve is for her to question God's Word; He places doubt in her mind.

The serpent went on to say, "*You surely shall not die. For God knows that in the day you eat from it your eyes will be opened and you will be like God, knowing good and evil.*" In other words, he was saying, God does not mean what He says!

He then appeals to her flesh by telling her she can be *like* God. He lies to her and she *believes* him.

---

[24] Robert Lewis, *The New Eve* (Nashville: B&H Publishing Group), 2008.

Eve then looks at the tree, comes up close to the tree, smells the apples, desires them, takes, and eats. She proceeds to hand one to her husband, Adam, and he eats it.

We may think we can hide our sins from God, but He sees all; nothing is hidden from Him. Adam and Eve's fellowship with God was then broken, just as it is when we sin; our sin separates us from God.

God comes looking for them and calls out to Adam. He responds to God by saying, *"I was afraid because I was naked; so I hid myself."* Ooops! How did Adam know that?

God asked him, *"Who told you that you were naked? Have you eaten from the tree of which I commanded you not to eat?"*

Then the Blame Game begins, *"Lord, actually it was the woman YOU gave me."* Then God turns to Eve and asked what she had done. She responds, *"The serpent made me do it."* Thus the expression, "The devil made me do it."

God then curses the serpent, and pronouncing punishment on Eve, he tells her that He will greatly increase her pain in childbirth and her husband would rule over her.

I think the most powerful verse is Genesis 3:17, NASB: *"Then to Adam He said, 'Because you have **listened** to the voice of your wife, and have eaten from the tree about which I commanded you saying, "You shall <u>not</u> eat of it," cursed is the ground because of you; in toil you shall eat of it all the days of your life.'"*

Dianne's Personal Testimony: (Leadership may want to share their own testimony related to wrongly influencing your husband.) *Like Eve, there have been times in my years of marriage when my husband has **listened** to me, and I have led him in the wrong direction or even caused him to sin. Over the past few years, God has brought to the forefront of my mind several instances when my attitude toward a person or a situation negatively impacted my husband's perspective toward that particular person or situation. Because I negatively affected him and because he **listened** to me, he did not have the opportunity to make an unbiased decision about the person or the situation.*

Women have the power to sway the men in their lives toward good or evil. These men trust us—as Adam trusted Eve—and we should guard that trust with the utmost integrity. A spirit-filled woman can be trusted!

Living a spirit-filled life does not mean *perfection*, because we are all human and prone to sin. But it does mean that we can make every effort to be godly, spirit-indwelled women, filling our minds and hearts with God's Word. If we know His Word, we will not be deceived, as Eve was.

We can also ask the Father to help us to be completely surrendered to the Holy Spirit's control in our lives. We often resist surrendering every part of ourselves to the Holy Spirit. Eve's flesh wanted its own way, and we often want our own way.

Galatians 5:16–22, NASB says, *"Walk by the Spirit and you will not carry out the desire of the flesh . . . But the fruit of the Spirit is love, joy, peace, patience, kindness, goodness, faithfulness, gentleness and self-control."*

For college/single young women, read the following scenario of a situation with a boyfriend. After reading, ask the young women in what way the young lady in this scenario should respond to the situation in order to wisely influence her boyfriend and not lead him in the wrong direction.

Scenario:

You and your boyfriend are going out for the evening with some friends. Earlier in the day, you are on the phone with one of the girls you're going out with. In the course of the conversation, she mentions that she and her boyfriend really don't like the fact that you and your boyfriend always choose the restaurant; they feel the two of you are cheap. If they are going out with you that night, they want to *choose* where the group will go. They would like some place nice without worrying about the cost. She informs you that if the group wants *them* to go, they are going to be the ones to choose.

At this point, you have one of two decisions to make:

Decision #1. After hanging up the phone, you fume all afternoon, mulling over every word your friend said during your conversation. As soon as your boyfriend arrives to pick you up, you begin to unload on him the anger and frustration you feel having listened to her insult the two of you. You criticize this other couple's extravagant spending habits. You defend your choices in restaurants. By the time you are finished, your boyfriend never wants to see these friends again. But because you have committed to go, and the third couple in the group is expecting you, you reluctantly go. The entire evening your boyfriend is upset and angry under the half smile he is displaying, and only you can tell just how mad he is. The night is ruined for him and for you. (This scenario takes place *only* if you choose not to text or call him immediately after talking to your friend, unloading on him while he is at work, which will affect his ability to concentrate on his work.)

Decision #2. While you are on the phone with your girlfriend, you begin to pray that God would help you respond in a Christlike manner and exhibit the fruit of the Spirit. You tell her how sorry you are that you and your boyfriend are always the ones to choose the restaurant. You tell her it would really be fun to go to the place of their choosing, and afterwards you would like for everyone to come back to your apartment for dessert. You hang up the phone and thank the Lord for helping you keep control of your tongue. You then ask Him to help you to forgive, to forget, and to love her. You do not pick up the phone and call your boyfriend to tell him all about the conversation. In fact, when he arrives to pick you up that evening, you do not mention the conversation at all. Instead, you tell him everyone is coming to your apartment after dinner for dessert and that you are looking forward to your night with friends.

For married young women, read the following scenario of a husband and wife. After reading, ask the young women in what way the wife in this scenario should respond to the situation in order to wisely influence her husband and not lead him in the wrong direction.

Scenario:

You and your husband are going out for the evening with two couples. Earlier in the day, you are on the phone with one of the girls you're going out with. In the course of the conversation, she mentions that she and her husband really don't like the fact that you and your husband always choose the restaurant;

they feel the two of you are cheap. If they are going out with you that night, they want to *choose* where the group will go. They would like some place nice without worrying about the cost. She informs you that if the group wants *them* to go, they are going to be the ones to choose.

At this point, you have one of two decisions to make:

Decision #1. After hanging up the phone, you fume all afternoon, mulling over every word your friend said during your conversation. As soon as your husband walks in the door, you begin to unload on him the anger and frustration you feel having listened to her insult the two of you. You criticize this other couple's extravagant spending habits. You defend your choices in restaurants. By the time you are finished, your husband never wants to see these friends again. But because you have committed to go, and the third couple in the group is expecting you, you reluctantly go. The entire evening your husband is upset and angry under the half smile he is displaying, and only you can tell just how mad he is. The night is ruined for him and for you. (This scenario takes place *only* if you choose not to text or call him immediately after talking to your friend, unloading on him while he is at work, which will affect his ability to concentrate on his work).

Decision #2. While you are on the phone with your girlfriend, you begin to pray that God would help you respond in a Christlike manner and exhibit the fruit of the Spirit. You tell her how sorry you are that you and your husband are always the ones to choose the restaurant. You tell her it would really be fun to go to the place of their choosing, and afterwards you would like for everyone to come back to your place for dessert. You hang up the phone and thank the Lord for helping you keep control of your tongue. You then ask Him to help you to forgive, to forget, and to love her. You do not pick up the phone and call your husband to tell him all about the conversation. In fact, when he arrives home that evening, you do not mention the conversation at all. Instead, you tell him everyone is coming to your place after dinner for dessert and that you are looking forward to your night with friends.

Eve *listened* to Satan, Adam *listened* to Eve, and their decision affected all of mankind. You, as a woman, are a *woman of influence*—your words and actions affect those around you; use your influence wisely!

"If you need wisdom, ask our generous God, and he will give it to you . . . But wisdom from above is first of all pure. It is also peace loving, gentle at all times, and willing to yield to others. It is full of mercy and good deeds . . . It shows no favoritism and is always sincere. And those who are peacemakers will plant seeds of peace and reap a harvest of righteousness" (James 1:5, 3:17–18, NLT).

Close in prayer.

Week Two Discussion Questions

- Who does the serpent approach? *Eve—the woman*

- What is the serpent doing? *Engaging her in conversation. She responds to his question and begins a conversation with the serpent. "From the fruit of the trees of the garden, we may not eat; but from the fruit of the tree which is in the middle of the garden, God has said, 'You shall not eat from it or touch it or you will die.'" She should have run, as I did!*

- Was it Eve that God spoke to when He said, "You are not to eat of the tree or touch it?" *No, it wasn't Eve, but Adam.*

- What was Eve's first mistake? *Her first mistake was that she engaged in a conversation with the serpent and took his word over God's Word.*

- What does this tell you about Satan? *He is a liar and a deceiver. He hates both God and man. He is very subtle.*

- Can man hide from God? *No! God is all-knowing and all-seeing. He is in all places at all times—omniscient and omnipresent God.*

- What was Eve's second mistake? *She wrongly influenced her husband, Adam.*

- Does the fact that Eve wrongly influenced Adam excuse him of his responsibility? *No! God placed Adam as the head. Before woman was created God gave Adam the first command, he was not to go near or eat of the fruit from the tree in the center of the garden. Adam obviously told Eve what God said because in her response to Satan she quotes God. "You may freely eat the fruit of any tree in the garden-- except the tree of the knowledge of good and evil. If you eat its fruit, you will surely die."*

- In what ways can women wrongly influence the men in their lives? *Discuss answers of class participants.*

- James 1:5 tells us that if we will ask for wisdom "our generous God" will give it to us. How can having God-given wisdom help in the area of a woman's influence over the men God has placed in her life? *Discuss answers of class participants.*

Kitchen Lingo

Week 3

Week Three: Kitchen Lingo

Week Three Lesson Plan

I. Leader opens in prayer

II. Devotional

Sarah—A Woman Unwilling to Wait. Read Genesis 12, 15:1–6, and 16:1–16 in order to prepare. (For help in preparing, refer to lesson outline in Devotional section of Leader Guide.)

III. Time in the Kitchen

- Introduce measurement. Have a variety of measuring cups and spoons for an illustration on measuring (glass for wet and metal or plastic for dry). Refer to handout entitled *Measuring Utensils for Cooking.*

- In order for the young women to experience measuring wet ingredients versus dry ingredients, make the *No-Bake Cookie* recipe. Recipe is included in this lesson. After preparing, refrigerate and chill. Finish lesson as follows:

- Weights and Measurement Chart. Using the chart, teach about equivalents. For illustration purposes, you may want to have clean empty containers/cartons on hand, for those who are visual learners. *For Example*: A gallon jug, two quarts of milk/half and half containers, four pints of heavy cream cartons, etc. Be creative! For fun, we have included a copy of the *Secrets* Gallon Girl chart.

- Use the *Kitchen Lingo Bingo* cards in introducing cooking terms. Beans or candy can be used as markers. Copy and cut sets of cards found in leader lesson. Pass out one play card per class student. From the *Leader's Lingo Bingo Answer Sheet*, read aloud each term. Class participants will place a marker on the word they feel matches. Once *Bingo* is declared, you may go back and read the words and terms aloud to make sure the answers of those declaring *Bingo* are correct. Emphasize the importance of knowing the definition of terms used in recipes you are planning on preparing. Optional: Have small prizes for winner, or winners, in case of a tie.

- If time allows, cover various cuts of meats, especially beef cuts. If desired: Google and copy grilling and cooking various cuts of meat charts for class participants. *For Example:* A rump roast versus a pot roast—tell about each and the process and time required for cooking each one. From a Web site listed, run off copies of the meat grilling/cooking chart for class participants. Laminate if desired.

- Homework assignment. On 3 x 5 index cards, write two grocery items. *For Example:* bread and Coke or blueberries and Tide detergent. Hand out one 3 x 5 card to each young woman; briefly explain comparison shopping. The students are to compare the price of their items in different stores or online and report their findings the following week.

- Prizes for the *Kitchen Lingo Bingo* game winner.

IV. Week Three Lesson Sheets

    INRODUCTION: *Floating in Syrup*
    KITCHEN LINGO BINGO SAMPLE GAME CARDS
    LEADER'S LINGO BINGO ANSWER SHEET
    SECRETS GALLON GIRL CHART—Teaching Measurements
    DEVOTIONAL: Sarah

V. Equipment for Week Three

- *Kitchen Lingo Bingo* cards, markers, and prizes for winners

- Ingredients needed to illustrate the cooking terms chosen by the leadership. *For Example*: A cut of meat for *Basting* and *Broiling* or vegetables for *Steaming* and *Roasting*. Paper plates, forks, and napkins to taste demo food

- Ingredients required for the preparation of the *No-Bake Cookie* recipe and plastic zipper-lock bags for transport.Cookie sheets, nonstick spray or parchment paper, quart saucepan, large bowl, spatula, large spoon, and enough measuring cups and spoons for each recipe (by coating the measuring cup with nonstick spray, demonstrate how to keep peanut butter and other sticky foods, such as honey, from sticking)

- Several different-sized containers for teaching/illustrating the *Weights and Measurement Chart*

- Package of 3 x 5 index cards with two grocery items listed on each card

Introduction: Floating in Syrup

Our two girls married within two years of each other. One of the first major decisions as a young married couple is which holiday to spend with which family. It is one of those *major* decisions that can often cause newlyweds to have their first major fight. Maybe some of you can relate. Mark and I had that fight! To be honest, when I was young and newly married, I was not fair to my in-laws. After all, I wanted to be with *my* family. Isn't it expected that the new groom will do whatever his new bride wants? I have, in my later years, regretted that I robbed my in-laws of time with their son. So, in an effort to make up for it, and because I did not want my girls to have the same regret, I encouraged them to be with us every other Christmas. The year they were at their in-laws for Christmas, we would make Thanksgiving our BIG holiday.

Our youngest daughter, Kelly, got married in August. So the girls decided that fall that they would go to their in-laws for Christmas. Due to their decision, we had to quickly plan our Thanksgiving and Christmas all in one. We considered several options: Would we have our traditional Christmas breakfast on Thanksgiving morning? Would we have turkey and the traditional Thanksgiving meal or serve something different? So many choices! We finally made our decision and put together our menu for Thanksgiving Day. We divided the responsibilities for cooking. Kelly was to prepare two items and one was going to be a dessert; she would decide just what dessert, once they arrived. On Wednesday before the BIG day, we set out to do all the cooking and baking with three little people under three around our feet. I was making a cake and a traditional pumpkin pie, so Kelly decided that a fruit pie would be good. Remembering how wonderful her mother-in-law's apple pie was, she called to get her recipe. Once that was in hand, she set out for the grocery store to purchase the ingredients. She was excited about her choice, since her dad loved fruit pie with ice cream, and this was a recipe she had never made before.

The crust was absolutely perfect and from scratch; no frozen crust for this pie! She worked hard slicing the apples and combining all the ingredients. Once the oven was preheated, she placed this beautiful pie in to cook. It smelled so good baking along with the turkey. After a while, she began to notice the syrup bubbling up and over the crust. We grabbed a cookie sheet to place under the pie, still bubbling and bubbling! Finally, the apples were cooked and the crust was a beautiful golden brown. She removed it from the oven only to discover that the apples were floating in syrup. Our first thought was that those were *really* juicy apples! But our second thought was, what went wrong? Kelly got out the recipe and began to read it. She then called her mother-in-law to go back over all the ingredients and their measurements. "Oh, that's it!" I heard her say. The recipe had called for a *half* cup of sugar and Kelly had written down *one and a half cups*—enough sugar for three pies! After the pie cooled, the apples were still *floating in syrup*. The three men in the family felt sorry for Kelly and each ate a piece.

We all laughed at the sight of that pie and Kelly learned a valuable cooking lesson that Thanksgiving—**accurate measuring is the key to the success of a recipe!**

Baste	Broil	Dice	Dredge	Marinate
Poach	Sauté	Bake	Au Jus	Braise
Coat	Grind	Fold	Fillet	Chop
Emulsify	Cube	Garnish	Julienne	Pickle
Shred	Grate	Boil	Whip	Puree

Kitchen Lingo Bingo Sample Game Cards

Copy and Cut for Activity

Zest	Pan Broil	Grind	Al Dente	Hull
Blanch	Whip	Clarify	Beat	Lukewarm
Gratin	Whisk	Bone	Deglaze	Flambé
Chill	Drizzle	Toss	Fry	Cream
Dash	Marinate	Braise	Dust	Panfry

Dredge	Baste	Coat	Shuck	Dice
Garnish	Dollop	Hull	Glaze	Al Dente
Beat	Clarify	Deglaze	Fold	Drizzle
Grate	Julienne	Knead	Pinch	Marinate
Puree	Roast	Sauté	Whip	Stew

Kitchen Lingo Bingo Sample Game Cards

Copy and Cut for Activity

Bake	Cure	Dust	Flambé	Boil
Flake	Batter	Degrease	Gratin	Lukewarm
Pare	Julienne	Blanch	Mince	Panfry
Filet	Broil	Dissolve	Cream	Stew
Caramelize	Poach	Fricassee	Scallop	Sear

Week Three Leader's Kitchen Lingo Bingo Answer Sheet

Read the definition only and wait for class participants to place marker on game board for the correct word. Then read the word along with the definition of the term. Move onto the next definition until you have a Bingo winner.

BASTE: To moisten foods during cooking with pan drippings or special sauce to add flavor and prevent drying

AL DENTE: Italian term used to describe pasta that is cooked until it offers a slight resistance to the bite

COAT: To dip or roll foods in flour, breadcrumbs, sugar, or a sauce until covered

DEGLAZE: To dissolve the thin glaze of juices and brown bits on the surface of a pan in which food has been fried, sautéed, or roasted. To do this, add liquid, stir, and scrape over high heat, thereby adding flavor to the liquid for use as a sauce.

BOIL: To heat a liquid until bubbles break continually on the surface

DRIZZLE: To sprinkle drops of liquid lightly over food in a casual manner

EMULSIFY: To combine, through a whisking action, two liquids that traditionally separate, such as oil and vinegar, into a uniform mixture

GRATIN: From the French word for *crust*. Term used to describe any oven-baked dish—usually cooked in a shallow, oval gratin dish—on which a golden brown crust of bread crumbs, cheese, or creamy sauce is form.

BEAT: To mix rapidly in order to make a mixture smooth and light by incorporating as much air as possible

MARINATE: To flavor and moisturize pieces of meat, poultry, seafood, or vegetables by soaking them in or brushing them with a liquid mixture of seasonings known as a marinade. Dry marinade mixtures composed of salt, pepper, herbs, or spices may also be rubbed into meat, poultry, or seafood.

PICKLE: To preserve meats, vegetables, and fruits in brine

PAN-FRY: To cook in small amounts of fat

WHIP: To beat rapidly to incorporate air and produce expansion, as in heavy cream or egg whites

STEW: To simmer slowly in a small amount of liquid for a long time

ROAST: To cook by dry heat in an oven

JULIENNE: To cut vegetables, fruits, or cheeses into thin strips

FOLD: To incorporate a delicate substance, such as whipped cream or beaten egg whites, into another substance without releasing air bubbles. Cut down through mixture with spoon, whisk, or fork; go across bottom of bowl, up and over, close to surface. The process is repeated, while slowing rotating the bowl, until the ingredients are thoroughly blended.

KNEAD: To work and press dough with the palms of the hands or mechanically, to develop the gluten in the flour

SAUTÉ: To cook and/or brown food in a small amount of hot fat

POACH: To cook very gently in hot liquid kept just below the boiling point

CARAMELIZE: To heat sugar in order to turn it brown and give it a special taste

DISSOLVE: To cause a dry substance to pass into solution in a liquid

FILET: A boneless cut of meat

FRICASSEE: To cook by braising, usually applied to fowl or rabbit

SCALLOP: To bake a food, usually in a casserole, with sauce or other liquid. Crumbs often are sprinkled over.

MINCE: To cut or chop food into extremely small pieces.

WHISK: A multi-looped, wire mixing utensil with a handle used to whip sauces, eggs, cream, etc. to a smooth, airy consistency. Also means to whip ingredients together.

FRY: To cook in hot fat. To cook in a fat is called pan-frying or sautéing; to cook in a one- to two-inch layer of hot fat is called shallow-fat frying; to cook in a deep layer of hot fat is called deep-fat frying.

FLAMBÉ: To flame foods by dousing in some form of potable alcohol and setting alight

CHILL: To cool foods to below room temperature (40°F or less), by placing them in the refrigerator, freezer, or an ice bath.

HULL: To remove the green stems and leaves of strawberries

BLANCH: To immerse in rapidly boiling water and allow to cook slightly

BONE: To remove raw or cooked meat from bones

CREAM: To soften a fat, especially butter, by beating it at room temperature. Butter and sugar are often creamed together, making a smooth, soft paste.

LUKEWARM: Neither cool nor warm, approximately body temperature

BRAISE: To cook slowly in a small amount of liquid in a covered pan on the stovetop or in the oven. Generally used for less tender cuts of meat.

CLARIFY: To separate and remove solids from a liquid, thus making it clear.

CURE: To preserve meats by drying and salting and/or smoking

DUST: To sprinkle food with dry ingredients. Use a strainer or a jar with a perforated cover, or try the good, old-fashioned way of shaking things together in a paper bag.

TOSS: To combine ingredients with a lifting motion

SHRED: To cut or tear in small, long, narrow pieces

PINCH: A pinch is the trifling amount you can hold between your thumb and forefinger.

PUREE: To mash foods until perfectly smooth by hand, by rubbing through a sieve or food mill, or by whirling in a blender or food processor

SHUCK: To remove the meat of oysters and clams from their shells. Also refers to removing the husk from an ear of corn.

BATTER: A mixture containing flour and liquid, thin enough to pour or thick enough to be dropped from a spoon

BAKE: To cook by dry heat, usually in the oven

PARE: To remove the outermost skin of a fruit or vegetable

GARNISH: To decorate a dish both to enhance its appearance and to provide a flavorful contrast. Parsley, lemon slices, raw vegetables, chopped chives, and other herbs are all forms of garnishes.

SEAR: To brown very quickly by intense heat. This method increases shrinkage but develops flavor and improves appearance.

DICE: To cut food in small cubes of uniform size and shape

STIR: To mix ingredients with a circular motion until well blended or of uniform consistency

WARM: To hold foods at a low temperature, usually around 200°F, without further cooking

SIFT: To put one or more dry ingredients through a sieve or sifter

GREASE: To rub the inside of a baking dish or pan with shortening, butter, or oil, or to coat with cooking spray to keep the contents from sticking

FILLET: As a verb—to remove the bones from meat or fish. A fillet is the piece of flesh after it has been boned.

DREDGE: To sprinkle or coat with flour or other fine substance

DEGREASE: To remove fat from the surface of stews, soups, or stock. Cool in the refrigerator so that fat hardens and is easily removed.

BROIL: To cook on a grill under strong, direct heat

At this point, you should have at least one Bingo winner. Stop game.

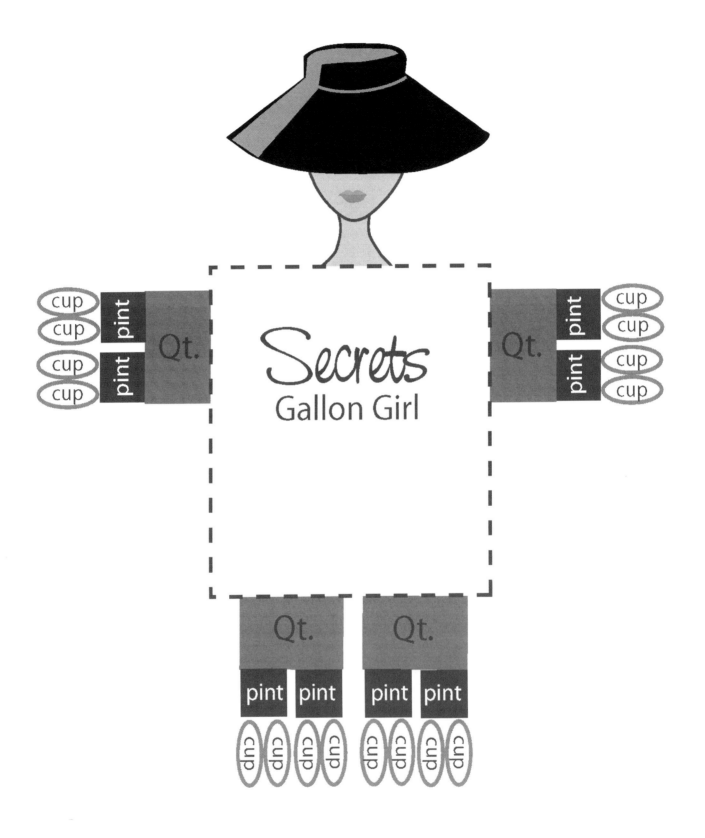

WEEK THREE: Sarah—A Woman Unwilling to Wait

Read Genesis chapter 12, 15:1–6, 16:1–16.

God tells Abraham that He is going to bless him and make him the father of many nations. When God told Abraham this, he did not have a son—an heir. In his mind, he must have wondered how God would keep His promise to bless and multiply his seed.

We see God calling Abram to *GO* forth; we see Abram's incredible act of faith and obedience in leaving his homeland. It says, *"And Abram went forth."* He took his wife, Sarah, and his nephew Lot—who was the potential heir since Sarah was barren—all their possessions, animals, and their entire household.

And you thought organizing your family for a long-distance move was a big task!

Abraham came up with his own plan for an heir in choosing Eliezer. He did not want to *wait* on God. *Chapter 15:2–3.*

We see God's patience with Abram. He does not scold him for coming up with his own plan but gently reminds him that He will keep His promise; Abram would have an heir that would come forth from his own body. His descendants would be as numerous as the stars. *Chapter 15:4–5.*

We, like Abraham, are guilty of doubting God's Word. We look around at our circumstances and forget that God is so much bigger than our circumstances. He also has a plan and a purpose for our lives; nothing will stand in the way of Him accomplishing those. *Job 42:1.*

Once again, we see the Blame Game that Adam and Eve played. Sarah blames Abram, and he puts the responsibility back on her. Neither was willing to *wait* on God.

What we see about Abraham:

- He was a weak leader in his home.
- He took his eyes off of God.
- He did not fully believe God's promise.
- He had his own plan.
- He doubted God.
- He listened to advice that seemed reasonable.

What we see about Sarah:

- She laughed at God.
- She did not trust God to fulfill His promise.
- She had her *own* plan—took matters into her own hands.
- She went from trusting to scheming and tried to take control.

- She misled her husband.
- She did not get the results she wanted.
- She despised Hagar and was jealous of her. (*There's not a more unattractive outfit on a woman than jealousy.*)

James 3:14–16, NASB, says, *"But if you have bitterness and selfish ambition in your heart, do not be arrogant and so lie against the truth. This wisdom is not that which comes down from above, but is earthly, natural, and demonic. For where jealousy and selfish ambition exist, there is disorder and every evil thing."*

Because of their unwillingness to wait, Ishmael was born.

A friend has often said to me, in regards to *waiting* on God, "You don't want to birth an Ishmael."

Iva May, in her W3 study,[3] says, "Not waiting on God always has negative and long-term consequences."

Iva goes on to state about God's promises, "When God gives a promise He generally allows much time to go by. What we believe about God determines what we do during the times of silence and *waiting*."

Isaiah 64:4, NASB, says, *"For from of old, man has not heard nor perceived by ear, neither has the eye seen a God besides You, who acts in behalf of the one who **waits** for Him."*

Dianne's Personal Testimony: (Leadership may want to share a testimony about a time in their own lives when they had to trust God and *wait* on Him.)

*My husband and I have been in what I would call a **school of waiting** for four years. We stepped down from our position at our church as executive pastor because we felt God was asking us to step down. Like Sarah, I immediately began to scheme. We had come from twenty years in the secular work force prior to entering the ministry eleven years before; I was determined we were going back. After all, we had made great **sacrifices** to be in the ministry, right? I thought we needed to replenish our savings and retirement plan. I set out to make sure we did just that. We had been through some very difficult circumstances in ministry—no more full-time ministry for me! In fact, I think my exact words were, "I will never do that again!" Can I just tell you that God had different plans!*

These are just a few of the things I did not count on:

- The depression Mark suffered with for nine months, a result of exhaustion and many sleepless nights over the course of a year and a half due to a church split
- His diagnosis of a rare condition called Cerebellum Atrophy, which affects his balance and speech, and is a degenerative disease
- The necessity of selling our home
- Living in four rental homes in five years
- Rejection after rejection of job applications and interviews, both secular and ministry
- Failed insurance tests for licensing. Mark had been licensed in numerous states over his twenty years in the business, so there was no reason he should have failed from man's perspective, but he did!

---

[25] Iva May, *W3: Woman, Worldview and the Word* (Chronological Bible Discipleship), 2007. Revised 2010.

- The necessity of beginning a cake business and a painting business, along with God's call to begin this ministry

I thought I had it all figured out. But over these five years, God has taken me to a place I never ever dreamed of going. It has been very painful in so many ways, mainly because I resisted *waiting* on Him, and *trusting* Him with every aspect of our lives; I resisted living a life of total faith in a God who loved me and wanted only the best for me.

Not long ago, a friend said to me, "Dianne, it is what you do in the waiting time that counts. For it is in the waiting time that God does His greatest work."

I can honestly tell you that God did an incredible work in my life in those times of waiting. For out of that time of waiting God brought this ministry, along with numerous opportunities for Mark and me to testify to others of His faithfulness and goodness. He has given us a ministry of discipling young married couples. We have found Him to be a God who keeps His promises! He has promised to never leave us or forsake us, and He has not.

He promises to feed us and care for us, as He does the lilies of the valley and the birds of the air, and He has!

For the woman who said, "I will never do this again," I find it quite amusing that Mark and I are doing more ministry than ever before; God certainly has a sense of humor! I was a woman who was not willing to wait, a woman who had her own plan. God was patient with me. He had a plan and as it says in Job 42:1, *"Lord, I know that you can do all things and that no plan of yours can be thwarted."* He is fulfilling His plan for my life, and it is so much better than mine!

God had a plan for Abraham and Sarah. He had given them His promise, which He fully intended to keep. He always keeps His promises. But Sarah grew impatient and wanted her own way. Her decision affected not only her, but Abraham, Hagar, Ishmael, Isaac, everyone close to them, and ultimately all of mankind.

So, when God says:

Wait on Me to lead you to the right college, are you willing to wait?

Wait on Me for a husband, are you willing to wait?

Wait on Me for a house, are you willing to wait?

Wait on Me for a baby, are you willing to wait?

Wait on Me for a job, are you willing to wait?

Wait on Me for healing, are you willing to wait?

In her book, Iva May, author of *W3*[26] says, "God is more interested in our character development than our personal happiness."

Over these four years, my husband has said to me numerous times, "Dianne, God is much more concerned with our *being* than our *doing*."

Donna Gaines, noted author and Bible teacher says, "God does not need our help, only our cooperation."

It is in the waiting that God works His plan, His purposes, His design, and His will in us. Are you willing to wait on Him?

Close in prayer.

---

[26] Iva May, *W3: Woman, Worldview and the Word* (Chronological Bible Discipleship), 2007. Revised 2010.

Week Three Discussion Questions

- What had God promised Abram? *Chapter 15—An heir*

- Is Abram willing to wait on God to give him an heir? *No*

- What other man have we seen in the Bible who listened to his wife to his detriment? *See Genesis 3:17 and Genesis 16:2—Adam*

- What does Sarah do in her barrenness? *She gets impatient and decides to take charge of things herself. She thought, "I'll handle this." She did not want to wait on God.*

- Have you ever decided that God had forgotten you, and so you stepped in and took control of things? *Sarah concluded that God was not going to fulfill His promise, so we see her taking things into her own hands. She goes from trusting to scheming—such a female thing to do!*

- What does Sarah see as her only solution to her problem? *Her solution is her Egyptian maidservant, Hagar. Sarah gives Hagar to Abram as his concubine, he sleeps with her, and she conceives. We see things going from bad to worse for Sarah.*

- What got Abraham, Sarah, and Hagar into this situation? *Sarah and Abraham's unwillingness to wait on God and believe His promise.*

Questions to Ponder

Is God asking you to wait on something?

Are you surrendered to the wait or are you scheming and trying to have your own way because the waiting is too hard?

Is what God is requiring of you in the waiting more than you are willing to give?

Are you willing to let God do what He desires in your life while you wait?

Will He find you patient in the waiting or will He find you doubting and scheming?

If God is asking you to wait on something specific, will you cooperate? Will you surrender and trust Him? Will you wait on Him for His best

Week 4

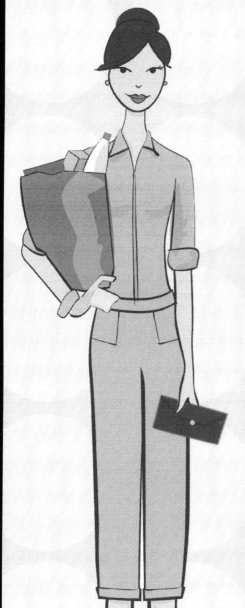

Not Another Trip to the Grocery Store!

Week Four: Not Another Trip to the Grocery Store!

Week Four Lesson Plan

I. Leader opens in prayer

II. Devotional

- *Hagar—A Woman of Submission*. Read Genesis chapter 16 in order to prepare. (For help in preparation refer to lesson outline in Devotional section of Leader Guide.)

III. Lesson—Choose one or all of the topics below for today's lesson according to the time allotted for class.

- Discuss the price comparison cards given as homework and the importance of price comparisons—the money that can be saved! Teach on couponing. You may want to invite a guest to come and share with the class the topic of couponing. Allow your guest the first hour and save the second hour for *Time in the Kitchen*. If leadership feels qualified, they may want to teach couponing.

- Cover meal planning by bringing in an expert to teach in Week Four or Week Five. Perhaps a young woman in your church/area who is especially gifted at meal planning and organizing; you may want to ask her to come and share her ideas with the class. Allow guest first hour and save the second hour for *Time in the Kitchen*. Look over meal-planning charts included in this week's lesson. Students can also copy free printable meal-planning charts and grocery shopping charts by going to www.organizedhome.com.

- Cover meal planning by having leadership share what they've learned in their vast years of experience in regards to planning meals. Teach the importance of meal planning in regards to grocery shopping. Point out that if you are organized in meal planning and use easy meals, with fewer ingredients, your grocery shopping will be less stressful and less damaging on the budget. Refer to iPhone apps available for recording grocery lists.

IV. Time in the Kitchen

- Using a roasted chicken, the young women will taste three *Quick and Easy* meals. The recipe for the chicken pizza will be prepared by the young women and the two additional recipes prepared ahead of time by the leadership. See *Chicken Pizza with Alfredo Sauce*. Have the crust and all the ingredients ready when the young women arrive in the kitchen. Demonstrate how to make the white sauce for the pizza. There are two white sauce recipes in the book; explain that the thin sauce can be used as a gravy, or you can add cheese to it and make macaroni and cheese, along with other dishes. The sauce for the pizza is a little thicker, enabling you to spread it on the crust. <u>Note</u>: What makes the sauce thicker or thinner will depend on the amount of flour in the recipe. Once sauce is cooked, let the young women assemble the pizza.

- While the pizza is cooking, demonstrate how to make gravy, using the thin, white gravy recipe or your favorite beef or chicken gravy recipe.

- Show the *Slaw Salad with Chicken* and the *Oriental Chicken Cashew Salad*; explain how they were made. Both are easy and quick. <u>Note</u>: Refer to other easy recipes in this week's lesson.

- Once pizza is cooked, serve all three recipes to the young women. <u>Note</u>: Costco® sells roasted chicken in vacuum-packed packages containing all-white breast meat for $10. This package can be subdivided and frozen for easy meals. This package is sufficient for all three recipes prepared today.

- Girls share their *Quick and Easy Meals*. Have the young women share their quick and easy meals with the rest of the class while tasting the recipes prepared today.

- *Dianne's Quick and Easy Meal Idea*: Purchase a bag of *Alexia*® brand potato dishes found in the freezer section of the grocery, some grocery stores have them in the Healthy Foods freezer section (found at your local *Fresh Market* stores). There are a variety of flavors such as Sauté Sweets, Harvest Sauté, Italian Sauté, and Sauté Reds. Each package has a different type of potato and vegetable mixture, complete with an olive oil and seasoning packet. In large skillet, sauté ¼ cup diced purple onion and 2 tablespoons minced garlic in 2 tablespoons olive oil. Once onion is tender, add seasoning packet and potatoes with vegetables. Heat on medium until cooked through, stirring occasionally. These are great side dishes for a meat entrée or add sliced turkey or chicken sausages/kielbasa for a complete meal. If adding the meat to the dish, brown the meat with onion and garlic, then add potato vegetable package, place lid on skillet, and cook until tender, stirring every 5 to 8 minutes. Enjoy your Easy Meal! Serve with side salad or all by itself. Each dish is full of vegetables for a balanced meal.

- Door prizes

V. Week Four Lesson Sheets

   INTRODUCTION: Hot Dogs and Bean with Bacon Soup
   DEVOTIONAL: Hagar

VI. Equipment for Week Four

- Ingredients for making the white sauce and the *Chicken Pizza*, as well as the ingredients for making gravy. A saucepan, wooden spoon, and measuring equipment. The choice for the flavor of gravy is left to the leadership. Prepared *Slaw Salad* and *Oriental Chicken Cashew Salad* along with dressing for each. The meat from two to three roasted chickens, chopped or diced, added to the salads. Plates and forks for tasting meals

- Have a jar of Classico® Alfredo Sauce to show that it can be substituted for the homemade white sauce

    - If desired, show packages of the Alexis potato dishes—one of the leaders may want to prepare a meal the week prior to Week Four using one of the varieties offered by Alexia and report to the class her results and what her husband/family thought of the *Easy Meal* using the Alexis potato dish.

Introduction: Hot Dogs and Bean with Bacon Soup

Mark and I married in 1973 at the ages of twenty-two and seventeen. The day after our wedding, we left Nashville, Tennessee, for South Florida, where Mark was working. I would imagine about now you are asking, what could a seventeen-year-old girl have known about homemaking? Not much! My grocery shopping and meal-planning experience, in particular, were at a minimum. Like most teenagers, I had run to the store for my mom, but as far as planning meals and doing the main grocery shopping, I was inexperienced! Week after week, we would go to the grocery store. Yes, I said *we*. He enjoyed going with me, but I will tell you, that is no longer the case. When we were first married, he enjoyed going and, after all, we couldn't be apart! I truly believe we spent twice as much as we do now, and when it came to meal planning that first year of marriage, *hot dogs and bean with bacon soup* were my specialties. That was about as creative as it got. Sounds good, huh? I have learned over the years that if I plan our meals for the week, my grocery shopping is much easier, and I save money buying only what I will need that week.

Girls, let's face it, grocery shopping is not much fun and can often be very frustrating, especially if you go without a list or a plan in mind. Have you ever walked into the grocery store without a list knowing there were things you needed, but you just couldn't remember what they were? Have you ever walked in the door and thought to yourself, *Now, why am I here, and what is it I need?* When that is the case, what usually happens is that you get home to find you just purchased your third bottle of mustard, but you forgot the detergent you have needed for a week.

When we are prepared and have planned ahead, it takes the frustration out of grocery shopping. Well, some of the frustration! Speaking of frustration, years ago I was checking out in a local grocery store; that particular week, I had a great deal of coupons. I got in line with my cart loaded down with groceries and only twenty minutes to get checked out and to the school to pick up the girls. Of all the days to get a new checker! He was a cocky, young teenager who was not at all happy about my coupons. I wasn't even what they call these days an "extreme couponer." Basically, I used coupons for cereal, cleaners, paper products, and a few other regularly purchased items. I handed the young man the stack of coupons and he proceeded to ask me if I had purchased all these items. I tried not to get offended that he was questioning my integrity, and graciously answered, yes. He waited until all the items had been scanned and bagged, then looked at me and said he would have to check to see that I had purchased all the items. The grocery industry has made great strides since then; now the computer will refuse a coupon if you have not purchased the product. But back then, it was up to the checker to make sure you had purchased every item. He went bag by bag—my twenty minutes were totally used up! I was becoming more and more upset. In the end, I had purchased everything for which I had handed him a coupon. I left never wanting to step foot in a grocery store again; but then that would not be possible, would it? Because your family enjoys eating, you must go to the grocery store, like it or not. So, here we go . . . like it or not!

WEEK FOUR: Hagar—A Woman of Submission

Read Genesis chapter 16.

Biblical History—Ham and Shem were the two sons of Noah. From Shem, numerous sons were born, and to them, more sons. Ten generations after Noah, Nahor, in the line of Shem, had a son named Terah, and he had a son named Abram. *Abram* means "exalted father." Later, God changed his name to *Abraham*, meaning "father of a great number." He was called of God to leave his homeland, the Ur of the Chaldeans, and to go to Canaan. God appeared to him promising to multiply his descendants and make his name great. We see a long line of obedience in this family tracing back to Noah, who, when God asked him to build an ark, obeyed. Abram obeyed and set out on the 1,500-mile journey with Sarai, his wife, Lot, his nephew, and all their household belongings, along with cows, goats, and sheep. God appeared to Abraham a second time and again promised to give the land of Canaan to Abraham and his descendants. Then Lot and Abraham separated. We see God's promise of an heir for Abraham, but he did not believe God would bless him with a son at his old age. He became impatient and decided he needed to adopt Eliezer as a son in order to have an heir for his estate. God told him NO! I don't need your help. You are to wait and trust me. I will give you an heir from your old, worn-out body. Wait and watch! Abraham told Sarah that God was going to give them a son, and she laughed. After some time, she grew impatient and decided to take matters into her own hands. She gave her Egyptian maidservant, Hagar, to Abraham as his concubine, whom she acquired when they took a side trip that God never intended for them to take into Egypt. Hagar conceived and gave birth to a son, Ishmael, Abraham's first son at the ripe, old age of eighty-five. Oh boy, was Sarah upset and jealous! This is where we pick up the story.

Sarah did not choose Hagar, but inherited her. It was her decision to give Hagar to Abraham.

The name *Hagar* means "immigrant" or "flight." She was an immigrant from Egypt, and we will see where the word *flight* fits into her story.

Sarah mistreated Hagar. As women, we can sympathize with Hagar's plight; she was a victim. Often in our society we see women who do not choose their circumstances but are actually victims of them. (*Leadership may have a modern-day example.*)

Sarah blamed Abraham for her grief. Not only was she not able to bear a son, but now the concubine *she gave* Abraham was pregnant with his first son. Blaming Abraham, she implied that it was entirely his fault.

"Then Sarai said to Abram, 'This is all your fault! I put my servant into your arms, but now that she's pregnant she treats me with contempt. The Lord will show you who is wrong—you or me!" (Genesis 16:5, NASB).

Sarah was playing the same game we have seen played before—the Blame Game. First, she blames Abram, and then she turns her frustrations and anger upon Hagar.

"So Sarah treated her harshly, and she fled from her presence" (Genesis 16:6b, NASB).

We see that Hagar took flight and it says, *"God sought after her."* I love that! *"Now the angel of the Lord found her."* He seeks after us, finds us, and longs to care for us.

The Lord called her by name. *"Hagar, Sarah's maid, where have you come from and where are you going?"* God calls us, His children, by name. He knows us.

Hagar answered the angel of the Lord and said, *"I am fleeing from the presence of my mistress Sarah."*

The angel said to her, *"Return to your mistress, and **submit** yourself to her authority."*

The word *submit* means "to give in to or surrender to another's authority." *Surrender* means "to yield possession or power, the act of surrendering."

Every human being wants to have control; some are prone to being more controlling than others, but we all struggle at one time or another with wanting to have control. Submitting is hard for us. The human flesh fights against it. In order to *submit* or *surrender*, we must be willing to let go completely.

Dianne's Personal Testimony: (Leadership may have your own testimony of a time when God was asking you to *submit* or *surrender* to His will and you resisted. Share it with the class.)

*Over the past four years of our journey, God has asked of me, over and over again, to surrender completely to His will for my life. Time and time again, I thought I had completely surrendered. But then the Holy Spirit would reveal to me that I was holding back. Several months ago, I came to a place of being so incredibly miserable in my resistance of the surrender God desired of me. One morning, in my time with the Lord, He brought to mind the picture of a game we played as a child. All day I thought about that game and how it related to my resistance in completely letting go, **surrendering** to the Lord. As kids, we would stand with our backs to a friend and the friend would say, "Just fall back; I will catch you." Then you would have to decide if you trusted your friend enough to completely let go and free fall backward into his or her arms. That afternoon, I was alone in the house and found myself on my face in our family room weeping before the Lord, broken over the resistance of my flesh to God's desire to have complete control of my life. As I was weeping, I felt Him say to me, "Dianne, stand and back up to the couch, now fall back, free fall. Let go completely—surrender." I know what you are thinking. She has lost her mind! I'll tell you, I did find myself looking around to make sure no one was in the house. It was all clear; after all, I was all alone! I stood, backed up to the couch, and just did a free fall, a full **surrender** into the couch. It was a picture of what my heavenly Father desired for me. I laid there and wept, asking God to forgive me for resisting a full surrender to Him. After several minutes, I went and washed my face, re-entered the family room, and turned on a CD already in the player. Pushing the play button, on came Michael W. Smith singing, "I **surrender** all, I **surrender** all, all to thee my blessed Savior, I **surrender** all." Wow! God had my attention! I am not certain how much you know about a CD player, but when you turn it on, the machine usually returns to the beginning of the song, not to the chorus. I began to cry again—female thing! I was amazed at how much God loved me, His child. He loved me so much that He arranged to have that particular chorus on just to remind me of what He desired for me—***to surrender all!***

The angel of the Lord told Hagar, *"Return to your mistress and submit (surrender) yourself to her authority."*

I can only imagine that going back to Sarah was the last thing Hagar wanted to do; yet she was submissive. She returned and surrendered to what God asked of her and to Sarah's authority over her.

Donna Gaines, a noted author and Bible teacher says, "Obedience equals blessing." We find this to be true in Hagar's life. She obeyed and God blessed.

"I (the Lord) will greatly multiply your descendants so that they shall be too many to count." The angel of the Lord said to her further, *"Behold, you are with child, and you shall bear a son; and you shall call his name Ishmael, because the Lord has given heed to your affliction."*

We see these words in the New Testament given to another woman who was willing to submit to God's will for her life—Mary. Matthew 1:18, NASB, says, *"... when his mother Mary had been betrothed to Joseph, before they came together she was found to be with child by the Holy Spirit."*

Luke 1:30–31, NASB, says, *"The angel said to her, 'Do not be afraid, Mary; for you have found favor with God. And behold you will conceive in your womb and bear a son, and you shall name him Jesus.'"*

God promises to bless Hagar for her obedience to what He asked of her in returning and submitting to Sarah, her mistress.

In her flesh, Hagar probably did not want to return to Sarah. Who would be willing to place themselves in a situation of being abused and mistreated?

God had revealed to Hagar that He was aware of her circumstances; she referred to him as Jehovah Roe—the God who sees. God knew her circumstances and would not leave her alone in them. If she surrendered, returned, and trusted Him, He would bless her and her descendants.

James 4:7a and 10, NASB, says, *"Submit therefore to God." "Humble yourselves in the presence of the Lord, and He will exalt you."*

Romans 12:1–2, NASB, says, *"Therefore, I urge you brethren, by the mercies of God; to present your bodies a living and holy sacrifice, acceptable to God, which is your spiritual act of worship."*

Close in prayer.

Week Four Discussion Questions

- Where did Hagar come from and how did Sarah acquire her? *Hagar was one of many gifts from Pharaoh in order to get rid of Abraham and his entire household. Abraham, fearing the famine and not trusting God to provide, headed for Egypt, where food was abundant. While there, he lied to the Egyptians about Sarah being his sister (told a half-truth—Sarah was his half sister). But a half-truth is a whole lie to God. She was beautiful and he feared they would kill him in order to get her. Once again, he did not trust God. So into Pharaoh's harem Sarah went. God kept Pharaoh from defiling her. He realized Abraham had lied and in order to get rid of him, Pharaoh gave him many gifts; among those gifts was a maidservant named Hagar.*

- How did Sarah respond to Hagar's being pregnant with Abraham's baby? *She was jealous and reduced Hagar to slave status; she was no longer Abraham's concubine.*

- What was Hagar's response to the cruel punishment of Sarah? *She took flight and fled to her homeland of Egypt. Here we see the other meaning of her name—flight!*

- Was God unaware of where she had been or where she was going? *"Where have you come from and where are you going?" No, He knew. God knows all things, but sometimes He asks us so that we have to acknowledge to Him where we are going and what we are doing. God is omnipresent (in all places at all times) and omniscient (all knowing.)*

Questions to Ponder

Why is it that we blame others when we take matters into our own hands, having made a bad decision because we are unwilling to wait on God?

Has there ever been a time when God asked you to submit to a situation, to certain authorities in your life, to His will, or His redirecting in your life? What was your response?

Has there been a time in your life when you resisted submitting, falling back into the Father's arms? What was the result of your unwillingness to submit?

Prayerfully consider these questions: Are you completely surrendered to the Lord? Is He the Savior and Lord of your life?

If you have accepted Him as your Lord and Savior, are you totally surrendered to whatever He would ask of you? To the plans He has for your life?

Are you willing to live in full surrender to the Savior? Will you surrender all, as Hagar did?

Week 5

It's 5:30. What's for Dinner?

Week Five: It's 5:30. What's for Dinner?

Week Five Lesson Plan

I. Leader opens in prayer

II. Devotional

- *Rebekah—A Woman of Deception.* Read Genesis 25:19–27 in order to prepare. (For help in preparing, refer to lesson outline in Devotional section of Leader Guide.)

III. Lesson

- Play the *Spice it up Game.* Have a variety of spices in small numbered but unlabeled containers. Pass them around. Allow the young women time to look, smell, and then write down which spice they believe each numbered container holds. The names of each can be placed on the bottom of the container. Once all the containers have been passed around, announce which spice each container holds and the best use for that particular spice. Check to see which young women have the greatest number accurate.

- If meal planning was not covered in Week Four, a meal planning expert can be brought in to teach on meal planning. Show meal planning charts to the class and discuss. Have young women share how they go about planning their weekly meals.

- Leadership may want to share their experiences in the area of meal planning; giving methods for accomplishing the task of planning meals in advance. Print out meal planning and grocery shopping charts or direct students to www.organizedhome.com for as many copies as they would like.

- The completion of today's lesson will take place in the kitchen.

IV. Time in the Kitchen

- Demonstrate how to make brewed tea. Refrigerate to serve with today's meal.

- The class will work together to prepare an easy meal. You may use the pasta recipe in the Leader Guide or select one of your own. When using the recipe provided in the book, divide the young women into groups of two to four, based on class size. Preheat kitchen oven to 400°F. Preheat outdoor grill, or if inclement weather, use a George Foreman grill. For main dish, use the Grilled Chicken Pasta with Roasted Vegetables and Pesto recipe. Have one group prepare chicken breasts on grill, another group cook the pasta, and another group slice the vegetables into approximately ¼ to ½-inch slices. Place them inside a large plastic zipper-lock bag containing olive oil, toss to coat, and place on cookie sheets to roast at 400°F. Once the grilled chicken breasts are cooked, have the young women cut into bite-sized pieces. Pasta should be drained and poured into a large bowl for tossing. Vegetable group stir vegetables during cooking process once or twice. Once vegetables are cooked, pour over the pasta along with chicken pieces and toss. Pour a jar of pesto over the top along with the cheese, toss, and serve. <u>Note</u>: Ideas for early preparation: The chicken can be grilled the night before. If you happen to be grilling hamburgers the night before, go ahead and throw the chicken on the grill. Chop and store in refrigerator once cooled. The vegetables can be roasted in the morning while the children are playing. Then all you will have to do at dinnertime is to cook the pasta, warm the vegetables and chicken in the microwave, add in pesto, cheese, toss, and serve with salad. Enjoy!

- If you are a single working woman and wondering how this recipe will work for you, the evening before you plan on serving this recipe, bake or grill the chicken breasts while preparing your entree for that evening. After you have eaten and are cleaning up, wash and slice the vegetables; place them in the oven to roast while you finish cleaning the kitchen. Once the chicken breasts and vegetables are cooked, cool and place in an airtight container. After arriving home from work the next day, prepare pasta according to the package. Warm chicken and vegetables in microwave, place in large bowl with the pasta, and toss. Add in pesto and cheese, serve with a salad. Enjoy!

- If the leadership desires to serve the salad and dessert recipes in today's lesson, divide young women accordingly in order to make the entree, the salad, and the dessert. Let the young women taste the meal.

- Tips on Freezing: While the young women are eating their easy meal, teach on freezing and other helpful tips for easy meal preparation. Refer to *USDA Fact Sheet on Freezing, Helpful Hints: Tips on Freezing, and the Teaching Notes on Freezing*.

- Meat Preparation. See teaching notes on meat preparation and freezing techniques. Illustrate how you can use a Reynolds Oven Bag when desiring tender, juicy chicken breast. First: Place four chicken breasts in baking bag and top with S&P, garlic powder, and ¼ cup chopped fresh onion (or frozen). Seal bag and bake at 325°F for two hours; meat will be very juicy. Let cool, remove meat from bones, and divide between two or three Ziploc® bags. Pouring a little of the juice over the meat in the bag, freeze to be used later in a soup or casserole. Second: Take one or two boneless chicken breasts, a meat mallet, two 1-gallon Ziploc® bags, and a bottle of your favorite marinade. Demonstrate *tenderizing* the chicken breast by placing them in one bag and using a meat mallet to tenderize. In second bag, pour in your marinade, place boneless chicken breasts in bag, and make sure each one is coated with marinade. Place in freezer. They can be thawed in refrigerator or in cool water bath, and it will marinate as it thaws. Grill or bake and enjoy!

- Leadership and class participants may want to share personal recipes with the class of Easy Meals they have used and then discuss the importance of having *Family Meal Time. See Leader Guide for sheet on Family Meals*.

- Make reference, if time allows, to *Eating Healthier: Making Healthy Meals* and *How to Read a Nutrition Food Label*.

- Door prizes

V. Week Five Lesson Sheets

    INTRODUCTION: It's Their Bread
    TEACHING NOTES ON FREEZING FOODS
    DEVOTIONAL: Rebekah

VI. Equipment for Week Five

- Small containers and spices for *Spice It Up Game*

- Brewed Tea: Saucepan, pitcher, large spoon, tea bags, sugar, and water

- *Grilled Chicken Pasta* Recipe—Ingredients for recipe. Cookie sheets for vegetables, two 1-gallon Ziploc® bags, olive oil, S&P, knives, cutting boards, meat mallet, grill/grilling equipment, large pasta pot, and a large bowl for tossing, onion, vegetables, chicken breasts, pesto, parmesan cheese, and pasta. *Tuscan Salad* and *Strawberry Trifle* optional. If prepared, in class, provide the ingredients for both recipes along with mixer, mixing bowl, wooden spoon, measuring cups, measuring spoons, rubber spatula, whisk, salad bowl, salad tongs, serving tongs or pasta serving spoon, and a trifle dish. Salad dressing: Serve either store-bought vinaigrette or lemon dressing called for in recipe. When preparing vegetables, demonstrate how to *roast* the vegetables and when preparing the salad, demonstrate how to *blanch* the green beans. Refer to the *Glossary of Cooking Terms* handout in Week Three

Introduction: It's Their Bread

My son-in-law has a nickname for me—The Freezer Queen. Apparently, when he was growing up, his mom froze very little. Since he entered our family, he has been amazed at all the things that I freeze. Just about everything goes in the freezer at some point. Shortly after our first grandchild was born, I was at my daughter and son-in-law's home. I was cleaning the kitchen when a loaf of bread on top of the refrigerator caught my eye. My first thought was, *That is going to dry out if it is left up there*. So, what did I do? Of course, I did the logical thing; I put it in the freezer to preserve it. That evening, once I arrived home, our phone rang and I heard, "Mom, what did you do with our loaf of bread?" If she had known me as well as I thought she did, she would have known the answer to that question! It was in the freezer, naturally. I told her that I was concerned it would dry out. My daughter let me know kindly, but in no uncertain terms, that *they* did not put *their* bread in the freezer. Mother-in-Law 101—do not put *their* bread that *they* bought in *their* freezer when you are at *their* house cleaning and caring for *their* baby! Seriously, I did learn a valuable lesson. I was in their home and their bread was none of my concern. I was not there to preserve *their* bread, but to be a help to my daughter and care for the baby. Oh, and did I say, clean *their* house?

Over the years, I have been amazed at how fascinated women are with the idea of freezing. Believe it or not, I have been asked several times to do a freezing talk and demonstration. Some women at our church are called upon to speak because of their deep insight into God's Word. They have been sought after to speak on topics such as prayer, disciple making, and mentoring. Not me, I am the *freezing* expert. I am still looking for the spiritual value in a freezing talk! God's Word does tell us to use our gifts; so if it is freezing, then tell others about freezing!

Teaching Notes on Freezing Foods[5]

- Freezing is a way of preserving food to be consumed weeks and months later.

- Most foods can be frozen, but not all foods freeze well; some may experience some deterioration of texture upon defrosting.

- Freezing does not lessen nutritional value; in fact, nutrients are retained better in frozen fruits and vegetables. Fresh produce begins to lose its nutrients as soon as it is picked. The sooner you freeze them, the better.

- Supermarket wrapping is good for one to two months, but for the best quality, wrap individually and place in plastic freezer bags.

- Show different freezer packaging to the class: freezer plastic bags, Rubbermaid, etc.

- LABELING is crucial when freezing; always date frozen packages.

- Foods should not remain at room temperature longer than thirty minutes before freezing.

- Meat, fish, and poultry lose very little of their nutrients when frozen; they are mostly unaffected by the freezing process.

- Items that do not freeze well are emulsions. Cream, mayonnaise, and milk do not freeze well. Damaging by freezing may result in curdling or separation of liquids.

- Any food containing cream or custard, for instance cakes, trifles, or tarts, will not freeze well. Heavy cream that contains 40 percent fat will do well frozen.

- Fruits and vegetables with high water content do not freeze well; the change in their texture is extremely noticeable in thawing. *For Example:* lettuce, celery, strawberries, radishes, melon, cucumber, cabbage, raspberries, etc.

- Starchy vegetables such as potatoes, butter squash, pumpkin, corn, lentils, dried beans, peas, and chickpeas, freeze much better and there is little change in texture when defrosted.

- In prepared dishes, all flavorings intensify while in frozen conditions. It is best to leave out spices, including salt and pepper, until food is defrosted, or use sparingly.

- Foods such as lasagna and mac and cheese, which contain some form of liquid, will thicken during the freezing process, so prepare the dish with more liquid than normal.

- Large pasta dishes freeze well for two to three months. Baked pasta dishes are best frozen BEFORE cooking.

---

[9] *Secrets from the Southern Living Test Kitchens* (Oxmoor House Inc., 2002).

- It is best not to freeze foods that contain gelatin; they do not turn out very well. If possible, use arrowroot to thicken food intended to freeze instead of flour or corn flour. Foods that are thickened with arrowroot are perfect for freezing.

- Foods that freeze well are: all kinds of raw meat, poultry, game, fish, and seafood; they can all be frozen with little change.

- The longer products are stored in the freezer, the less their quality will be.

- Raw products will fare better in the freezer than cooked ones, due to moisture loss in the cooking process.

- Most companies *flash freeze* their vegetables and fruits within hours of picking, retaining nutrients, freshness, texture, color, and aroma. They are better nutritionally than those picked, packed, and driven hundreds of miles.

- Fresh fruits and vegetables keep frozen for six to eight months.

- All types of bread can be frozen and kept for up to three months. Do not let air or moisture enter the packages; this will cause freezer burn.

- Freezer burn occurs after an extended time of not being sealed properly; there is no health risk with freezer burn.

- When freezing, get as much of the air out of the package as possible. The Food Saver machine works well.

- Pies freeze well, cakes and cookies too, if wrapped well.

- Can freeze butter, up to eight months, if sealed well.

- Soups freeze well, as long as they are not cream based or have sour cream, eggs, or mayonnaise.

- Tomato sauce freezes well. Stock-based soups and dishes also freeze well.

- Eggs? Yes, eggs can be frozen, but only outside their shells; store in an airtight container. If eggs are frozen in the shells, they will burst.

- Herbs can be frozen. The best fresh herbs for freezing are basil, dill, mint, oregano, sage, lemongrass, chives, tarragon, rosemary, and thyme. They will be soggy and lose texture but not flavor; best used in soups and casseroles but not as a garnish.

- Cooked rice can be frozen. Often in cooking, rice is left over and we wonder what to do with it. Leftover rice can be placed in zipper-lock bags or in small CorningWare® dishes and frozen for later meals. Remove from freezer, heat in microwave on defrost, or place it in a heat-proof dish in the oven at 350°F until thawed and warmed through. I place the frozen rice in a CorningWare® dish directly from the freezer and let it cook while the main entrée is cooking. By the time the entrée is done, the rice is warmed and ready to serve.

THAWING:

- Refrigerate frozen meats and casseroles twenty-four to forty-eight hours until completely thawed. Food thawed in the refrigerator can be safely refrozen without changing taste or quality.

- For thawing, allow eight hours per pound of meat, four hours per pound of poultry, and six hours per pound of fruits and vegetables.

- Fast thaw: place frozen package in airtight, watertight, sealed bag and cover with cold water. Change water every thirty minutes until completely thawed. Thawed foods will need to be cooked immediately.

- For microwave thawing, remove all wrapping. Dangerous chemicals will be released into food in the thawing process from wrappings. Allow six to eight minutes per pound of food on low setting in microwave.

- Foods lower in moisture, such as bread, cakes, cookies, etc. can be thawed at room temperature.

- To reheat frozen food without thawing, bake at temperature called for in the recipe and double the bake time.

WEEK FIVE: Rebekah—A Woman of Deception

Read Genesis chapter 25:19–27.

Liz Curtis Higgs in *Bad Girls of the Bible*[6] refers to Rebekah as, "Becky, a girl gone bad. We see in chapter 25 that Rebekah starts out good—seeking God—but somewhere along the way she goes bad.

Many of us start out well in our Christian life—desiring to do well, seeking after God—and then before we know it, we are in trouble. We have taken a wrong turn we begin to go bad.

Let's take a look at Rebekah's life and see if we can learn from her what the warning signs might be—that if adhered to—would keep us from going bad.

Before we begin, it might be good to take a look at the history of Isaac. *"Now these are the records of the generations of Isaac, Abraham's son: Abraham became the father of Isaac; and Isaac was forty years old when he took Rebekah, the daughter of Bethuel the Aremean of Paddan-aram, the sister of Laban the Armean, to be his wife. Isaac prayed to the Lord on behalf of his wife, because she was barren . . ."* (Genesis 25:19–21).

We see God answering Isaac's prayers. *". . . and the Lord answered him and Rebekah his wife conceived."*

Once Rebekah conceived, there was a struggle going on within her womb. She was concerned about what she was feeling and needed to know what was happening within her womb.

She obviously recognized that God had allowed her to conceive, and only He could tell her what was happening within her womb.

Read Genesis chapter 25:21–26.

This difficult relationship between her sons was a picture of what was to come—the eventual struggle between the Edomites and the Israelites, the lineage of Esau and Jacob.

In Genesis 25:27–28, we see where Becky begins to go bad. It says, *"When the boys grew up, Esau became a skillful hunter, a man of the field, but Jacob was a peaceful man, living in tents. Now, Isaac loved Esau, because he had a taste for game, but Rebekah loved Jacob."*

The point at which Becky began to go bad was when she favored one child over the other. Not good! Because she did, she was unable to be fair and balanced in her treatment of her sons.

In verses 29–34, we see Jacob taking advantage of Esau's hunger and Esau failing to hold with respect and honor the birthright that was his as a result of being the firstborn. So what was rightfully his, Esau gave away because his stomach was growling.

---

[27] Liz Curtis Higgs, *Bad Girls of the Bible and What We Learn from Them* (Colorado Springs: Waterbrook Press, 2000).

Biblical History— *"The birthright of the eldest son gave him precedence over his brothers and assured him a double share of his father's inheritance. It could be forfeited by committing a serious sin and it could be bartered, as in this instance. The agreement was solemnized by an oath, see verse 33"* (Genesis 25:31–33, NAS Ryrie Study Bible).

Read chapter 26 where you will see that, once again, a famine takes place in the land.

Isaac left to look for food in Egypt (sound familiar?). The Lord appeared to Isaac and told him to stay put and *trust* Him; the Lord would take care of him and his family. *"I will be with you and bless you."*

Isaac's father, Abraham, failed to *trust* God; he took the family to Egypt and got into a little trouble there. So Isaac stayed put and trusted God.

God gives Isaac a promise to multiply his descendants and bless them. God always keeps His promises!

In chapter 27, we see that Isaac is very old, his eyes too dim to see. He called his oldest son, Esau, to his bedside. *"My son."* And he said to him, *"Here I am."*

Isaac tells Esau that he is old and his death certain. He asks him to go hunt game in order to prepare a savory dish for him, after which, he would give the blessing to his son, Esau.

At this point, Becky goes from bad to worse. *"Rebekah was listening while Isaac spoke to his son Esau."*

In other words, she was eavesdropping. Again, because she loved Jacob more, she was going to look after his interest. *"Rebekah said to her son Jacob, 'Behold I heard your father speak to your brother Esau, saying, "Bring me some game and prepare a savory dish for me, that I may eat, and bless you in the presence of the Lord before my death."'"* Now we see her going from eavesdropping to deceiving.

Rebekah's deception begins. *"Now therefore, my son, listen to me as I command you."* She proceeds to instruct Jacob in how to deceive his blind father into believing he was Esau. Jacob questions her as to whether or not the plan would work, and she assures him it would. *"Your curse be on me my son; only obey my voice, and go get them for me."*

Here we see a mother, Rebekah, leading her son into deception; she has really gone bad!

Jacob does everything his mother instructs him to do.

Rebekah had a plan. She provided all Jacob needed to deceive his father and encouraged him to lie. She was a bad girl!

Let's look at Jacob's lies:

Lie #1 Jacob went to his father dressed like Esau, smelling like Esau, with a savory dish in hand. Isaac questioned him about the quickness of getting back to him. Jacob said, *"Because the Lord your God caused it* *to happen to me."*

Isaac ignored his God-given senses. *"The voice is the voice of Jacob, but the hands are the hands of Esau."* Ignoring what he sensed was Jacob's presence, he proceeded to bless him: *"so he blessed him."*

Lie #2 Isaac asked him, *"Are you really my son Esau?" And he said, "I am."*

At Isaac's request, Jacob brought the food and wine to him to enjoy. This time, Isaac relied upon his sense of smell to make a judgment as to which son was standing beside him. *"So he came close and kissed him; and when he smelled the smell of his garments, he blessed him and said, "See, the smell of my son is like the smell of the field which the Lord has blessed; now may God give you the dew of heaven, and of the fatness of the earth, and an abundance of grain and new wine; may peoples serve you, and nations bow down to you; be master of your brothers, and may your mother's sons bow down to you. Cursed be those who curse you, and blessed be those who bless you."*

With his father's blessing, Jacob left, and quickly, I would imagine!

Just moments later, Esau arrived back and prepared his savory dish for his father. He stood before him and said, *"Let my father arise and eat of his son's game, that you may bless me." "Esau,"* his father said to him, *"Who are you?" And he said, "I am your son, your firstborn, Esau."*

Isaac realized that it was Jacob who had come and taken away Esau's blessing. It was too late; nothing could change what had happened.

Rebekah paid a great price for her deception and for leading her son in deception against his father and brother. She was a girl who started out good, but went bad.

Let's look at what happened to cause Becky to go bad:

- She gave way to sin; she loved one son more than the other.
- Then she *eavesdropped* on a conversation that was none of her business.
- She took matters into her own hands; she *schemed* to make sure Jacob received his father's blessing.
- She led her son in *deceiving* his father.
- She *lied* to Isaac about her desire for a bride for Jacob, so that he could receive Isaac's blessing on going to Haran, Rebekah's homeland. The reason for Jacob's leaving was not to get a bride but to escape his brother's fury.

Now that is quite a list, and it started with one seemingly small sin!

Sin is progressive; it starts with something seemingly small but leads to big consequences.

What were the consequences of Rebekah's sin?

- Sibling rivalry

- One son hated the other and wanted him dead. *"So Esau bore a grudge against Jacob."*
- She was separated from the son she loved so much. *"Then Isaac sent Jacob away."*
- She lost both sons in the process.
- Her son and her husband would never be able to trust her again.
- Her sin separated her from God.

Becky started out good; she was a seeker after God, but gave way to sin and ended up on the list of bad girls of the Bible. She was a deceiver and a schemer. The end does not always justify the means! Close in prayer.

Week Five Discussion Questions

- What do Sarah and Rebekah have in common? *They were barren women and both had to rely on the Lord to bless them with children.*

- Who petitioned the Lord on behalf of Rebekah? *Her husband, Isaac*

- Rebekah sensed a struggle within her and went to inquire of whom? *God*

- What was the reason God gave for the struggle within her womb? *"Two nations are in your womb; and two peoples shall be separated from your body; and one people shall be stronger than the other; and the older shall serve the younger."*

- Rebekah gave birth to twins. What were their names? *The firstborn was Esau; his name means hairy. The second was holding onto Esau's heel. He was Jacob; his name means heel catcher or trickster.*

- What lie do we see Isaac repeating? *He lied about Rebekah to Abimelech as his father did about his mother, Sarah, saying she was his sister. He, like his father, feared for his life. Apparently, both men had great taste in women. These ladies were so beautiful, their husbands feared other men would kill them in order to have their wives.*

- How does Rebekah solve the problem of Esau being a hairy man and Jacob being a smooth man in order to deceive Isaac? *She covered him with goatskins.*

- In what ways can we deceive those we love? *1. By hiding shopping receipts from your husband, 2. When asked a question, you are not totally honest in your answer. What are some other ways?*

- What did Isaac realize when Esau re-entered the room with his feast? *That he had been deceived. He had given the blessing to another, the blessing that rightfully belonged to Esau.*

- What was Esau's reaction at finding out his blessing had been given to another? *"When Esau heard the words of his father, he cried out with an exceedingly great and bitter cry, and said to his father, 'Bless me, even me also, O my father.'" He began to cry and beg his father to bless him.*

Questions to Ponder

Have you ever noticed that one lie leads to another lie?

Are you living a life of deception?

Are you the type of woman who will do whatever it takes to get your own way?

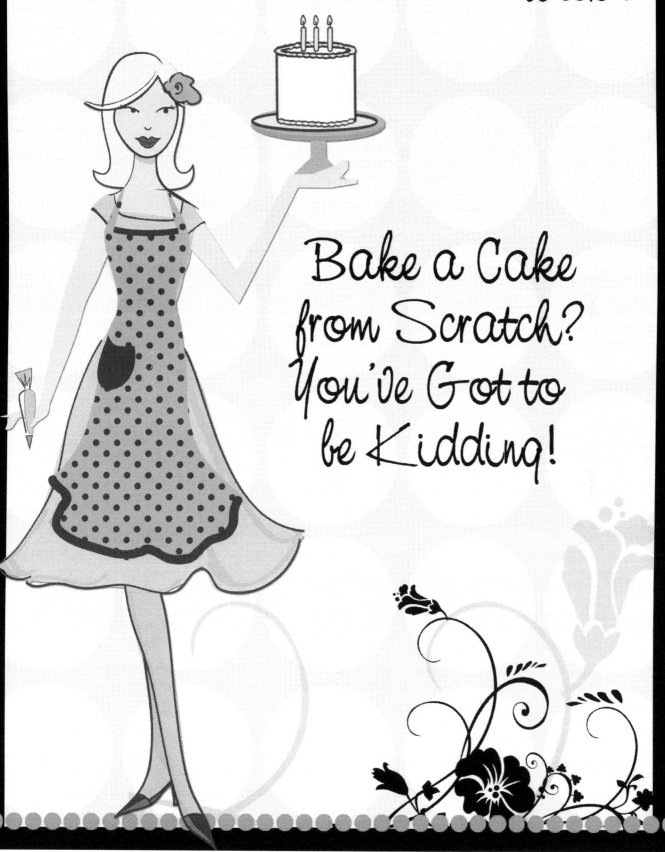

Week Six: Bake a Cake from Scratch? You've Got to Be Kidding!

Week Six Lesson Plan

I. Leader opens in prayer

II. Devotional

   Leah and Rachel—Women of Rivalry. Read Genesis chapters 28–30 in order to prepare. (For help in preparing, refer to lesson outline in Devotional section of Leader Guide.)

III. Lesson

- If the leadership chooses to prepare the cupcake recipe found in today's lesson, it will be best to prepare the batter and cook immediately following the devotional. The leadership not participating in the teaching of the day's lesson can oversee the baking of the cupcakes. At the end of today's lesson, the young women can be shown how to ice cupcakes with piping bags and tips using the recipe of buttercream icing or they may want to make and apply the *Seven-Minute Icing*. For piping made simple: bring a small Ziploc® sandwich bag, fill halfway with icing, cut corner tip, squeeze, and pipe onto cupcakes.
- Play the *Matchin' and Bakin' Game*. The young woman with the greatest number correct wins.
- After playing the game, demonstrate a few baking terms using baking utensils. *For Example: Sifting*—have a couple of different sifters on hand to show the girls, then sift flour and explain the necessity for sifting flour in some recipes. *Zest*—zest a lemon and explain how zest is used in recipes. *Egg wash*—Using a basting brush, water, and an egg, wash top of rolls. Explain what the egg wash does for the bread.
- Have a variety of bakeware and utensils specific to baking for the young women to view; explain usage of each. <u>Note</u>: Be sure to explain that glass and nonstick bakeware tend to cook faster; they may want to lower the temperature of the oven a few degrees when using these pans.
- Explain and demonstrate the procedure for prepping bakeware before using. *For Example:* Recipes that call for oil and flour coating. Refer to the *Basic Bakeware and Bakeware Substitutions* lesson sheet as a reference to use when the pan called for in a recipe is not available.
- Refer to the *Cooking and Baking Substitutions*. *For Example:* To substitute for corn syrup in a recipe, use 1 cup water and ¼ cup sugar. *Substitutions* were introduced at the beginning of the semester, if time is too short this week to discuss.

IV. Time in the Kitchen

- Make *Seven-Minute Icing* and using an angel food cake, demonstrate how to ice the cake, or prepare the *Butter Cream Icing* and demonstrate how to ice cupcakes (baked earlier) with a piping bag and large star tip.

Easy Cupcake Recipe

1 box devil's food cake mix, or butter flavor (I prefer Duncan Hines®)
1 cup buttermilk
Amount of oil called for on box
1 teaspoon vanilla
4 large eggs, room temperature

Preheat oven to 350°F. Mix in order of recipe. Fill paper-lined cups two-thirds full. Bake until toothpick inserted in the center comes out clean.

V. Week Six Lesson Sheets

    INTRODUCTION: Tapioca Pudding and Brownies
    MATCHIN' AND BAKIN' GAME
    TEACHING NOTES ON BAKING
    DEVOTIONAL: Leah and Rachel

VI. Equipment for Week Six

- Variety of baking pans and utensils set out to show muffin pans of various sizes, cake pans of various sizes, spring-form pan, Bundt pan, loaf pan, pie pan, cookie sheet, and utensils. Use oil and flour to demonstrate flour-coating a pan—this process is healthier than using aerosol nonstick spray
- Equipment for terms demonstration—will be determined by the baking terms chosen. *For Example*: a sifter
- Ingredients for substitution demonstration, should leadership decide to do a demonstration on substitutions
- Use an angel food cake to demonstrate icing a cake using the *Seven-Minute Icing*. Ingredients for *Seven-Minute Icing* or butter cream icing, ingredients for cupcake recipe, if making in class. Liners for muffin pan, double boiler for *Seven-Minute Icing*, wooden spoon, spatula, hand mixer, and spreader to ice cake. Cake stand, cupcake holder or round platter for cupcakes
- Prizes for *Matchin' and Bakin' Game* winners

Introduction: Tapioca Pudding and Brownies

As a child, my family had very little monetarily. My parents were both earning their graduate degrees in order to provide a better future for us. As busy as my mom was, she never neglected to keep our home, or cook and bake for us. Due to the lack of funds and having had four children, eating out at a restaurant wasn't an option. In fact, I do not remember eating out at a restaurant until I was in junior high school. We did have a few special treats at our house. One of my earliest memories was Saturday mornings when my mom would make fresh, hot, homemade donuts and dip them in confectioners' sugar or cinnamon sugar. We got to choose our coating; oh were they good! Another special treat was a trip to the local A&W Root Beer® drive-thru to purchase a gallon of ice-cold root beer. We took it home and Mom would pop some fresh popcorn on the stove; it slowly popped, kernel by kernel. Once the pan was filled to the brim with fresh popped corn, Mom would cover it in melted margarine. You see, butter was much too expensive. What a treat that was for us! Then there was my favorite *special treat*, which we were able to have on occasion—Mom's homemade brownies. I am talking from scratch! While the brownies were baking, Mom would prepare a saucepan of tapioca pudding. We always knew it was chilled and ready when it got a dark yellow film on the top. Mom would scoop it into individual bowls, topped with Cool Whip®, and serve it with a homemade brownie, yum! The Jell-O® brand does not hold a candle to Mom's homemade!

Another of my favorite *treats* as a child was my grandpa Barton's homemade chocolate syrup on top of his homemade vanilla ice cream, all from scratch! We would only get that special treat once or twice a year when my grandparents would visit. Just talking about these treats makes me want to be a child again. I can just taste them now! Being in the kitchen and creating something others will like is what I have enjoyed doing since I was a young girl. Just so you know, I am not Rachael Ray or Paula Deen, but I do love to cook and bake. I have found it interesting that of my two daughters, one enjoys cooking and the other daughter enjoys baking. Kelly loves to cook; she is always collecting new recipes. Her most-prized possession is her Sudoku knife and her nice thick wood cutting board. Jake and Josh get in on everything mom is making. Our older daughter, Angela, loves to bake; her children enjoy pulling up a chair to the mixer and making their favorite thing—poppy seed bread. Even before Angela was seriously dating anyone, she purchased her first Kitchen Aid mixer. It is fun for me to watch them both enjoy these aspects of being a homemaker and mom. They are making memories, just as my mom made for me. Oh, for some hot brownies and fresh homemade tapioca topped with Cool Whip®!

Matchin' and Bakin' Game

Batter — The stage of beating heavy whipping cream or egg whites so that when the beaters are lifted from the mixture, points stand straight up

Dollop — To swirl light and dark batters in a cake. It should not be combined to make one color; there should be two distinct colors

Dust — To pierce food or pastry with the tines of a fork to prevent them from bursting or rising during baking

Extracts — To heat milk or cream over low heat until just before boiling

Garnish — A small mound of soft food such as whipped cream or whipped topping

Knead — To lightly sprinkle with confectioners' sugar, baking cocoa, or flour

Marble — The distilled essential oils from plant materials, which dissolve in alcohol. Examples: vanilla and almond

Prick — An edible accompaniment used to decorate a dish for eye appeal, sometimes to boost flavor

Scald — A mixture made of flour and a liquid such as milk. It may also include other ingredients such as sugar, butter, oil, eggs, leaveners, and flavorings. Consistency ranges from thick to thin

Stiff Peaks — To work dough by using a pressing and folding action to make it smooth and elastic

For correct answers, see "Glossary of Baking Terms"

Week Six: Teaching Notes on Baking[7]

Follow these steps for successful baking:

- Read the recipe all the way through; this will minimize surprises.

- Prepare your ingredients ahead of time.

- Follow the recipe. It is your blueprint; follow it!

- Use good technique and execution; this is the key to success.

- Use the best and freshest ingredients.

- FLOUR: Recommend sifting or stirring before measuring. Always level with knife after scooping flour from container. <u>Types of Flour</u>: Unbleached all-purpose is naturally aged versus bleaching with chemicals. Whole wheat is ground or regular stone wheat. Comes in white whole wheat—King Arthur flour recommended.

- SUGARS: White granulated is pulverized a little finer. Brown sugar is granulated with traces of molasses; it adds a caramel taste and color. Confectioners' sugar has been pulverized with cornstarch. Honey is a source of sweetener but has to be watched closely because it goes quickly from golden brown to scorched.

- BAKING FATS: For butter, unsalted is best. When substituting butter in cakes, muffins, and quick breads, it is best to use canola, vegetable, corn, olive, and safflower oils. Shortening is a vegetable fat occasionally called for in pastries.

- EGGS provide flavor, color, leavening, and tenderness; use at room temperature. If you forget to take them out, place in a bowl, cover with warm water, let stand 20 to 30 minutes.

- WHOLE MILK is best in baking. It assists browning and tenderizing in baking; best at room temperature. Cream, depending on the recipe, can be substituted with half and half, whipping cream, or heavy cream. Evaporated milk can be substituted for half and half. When whipping cream is called for, use whipping cream. Buttermilk combined with baking soda produces an exceptionally light and tender baked good. Sour cream and yogurt are interchangeable in most recipes; sour cream is higher in fat.

- LEAVENERS help baked goods to rise. This includes: baking soda, baking powder, eggs, and yeast. Baking powder is baking soda mixed with cornstarch. Baking soda is simply soda and expired dates do not apply. Salt is used to counteract the sweetness in a recipe.

- FLAVORINGS add flavor to a recipe, vanilla being the most common.

- CHOCOLATE—The unsweetened variety is chocolate without any added sugar or vanilla. Unsweetened can be substituted for semisweet without adjusting the recipe. Milk chocolate contains liquor, added sugar, milk, and vanilla. White chocolate is made from cocoa butter or fat, milk, and sugar. Cocoa powder is pure chocolate and contains no cocoa fat.

- Spices need to be high quality to get high taste. Store in freezer or sealed container away from light.

---

[17] Marcy Goldman, *A Passion for Baking* (Oxmoor House, 2007).

WEEK SIX: Leah and Rachel—Women of Rivalry

Rebekah and Jacob deceived Isaac. Once deceived, Esau sets out to get revenge on Jacob for stealing his father's blessing, rightfully his as the oldest son. Fearing for the life of her son, Jacob, Rebekah lied to Isaac about the reason she wanted Jacob to head for her homeland. Jacob sets out for Haran to locate his mother's brother, Laban, and to find a wife! This is where we pick up the story.

Read Genesis chapters 28–30.

Jacob moved the stone from the well for Rachel and then kissed her, which was a proper greeting for cousins in that day and time. We then see him weeping; the reason for his tears was the joy he felt in finding his family.

"So it came about, when Laban heard the news of Jacob his sister's son, that he ran to meet him, and embraced him and kissed him and brought him to his house. Then he related to Laban all these things" (Genesis 29:13, NASB).

Laban recognized him as a relative and we see Jacob deciding to extend his visit for a month.

Read Genesis 29:13–14.

Then he was delayed because Laban changed the deal on him. Read Genesis 29:15–25.

The deceiver has been deceived! Jacob and his mother deceived his father and his brother, and now he is deceived. Looks like it runs in the family! See the principle of "you reap what you sow"

Laban explained to Jacob that it was not their tradition to allow the younger to marry before the firstborn. So Leah had to be given to Jacob out of tradition not because he loved or desired her, but because they had to abide by their traditions. Genesis 29:16–30.

Jacob was told he had to spend the traditional wedding week with Leah, and then he could have Rachel, but only in exchange for another seven years of service. Two wives in one week!

We are told Jacob loved Rachel more than Leah.

In Genesis 29:31, NASB, we see a picture of the mercy and compassion of God. *"Now the Lord saw that Leah was unloved, and he opened her womb, but Rachel was barren."* God remembered Leah and blessed her.

Dianne's Personal Testimony: *I have a friend, who for years was unable to have a baby. She and her husband taught a young married couples' class at our church. I have often wondered how she managed to attend all those baby showers and make the hospital visits when she herself so desired to have a baby, yet her womb was closed.*

Leah must have been filled with such joy at being pregnant with Jacob's baby. She thought, *"Now he will love me as much, if not more, than my sister, Rachel."*

At the same time, Rachel was filled with the pain of an empty womb. She must have wondered, *Will Jacob love Leah more than me because she has been able to give him a son?* Genesis 29:31–35.

Birth Announcement #1: It's a boy!

It would appear that Leah was trying to rub it in Rachel's face, as the saying goes. Women can be so spiteful.

Leah surmised that God saw her agony in not being loved by her husband and was merciful to her, in giving her a son.

She conceived again. Birth Announcement #2: It's a boy! She named the second son Simeon; his name means "hearing." God knew she was unloved, and He heard her prayers.

Birth announcement #3: It's a boy! Leah named him Levi, which means "attachment." She just knew that after bearing Jacob three healthy boys, he was going to be attached to her; in other words, he was going to finally love her.

We see the rivalry of two women: one desiring to be loved by her husband in the same way he loved her sister, and the other desiring to bear her husband a son as her sister had done for him.

Birth Announcement #4: It's a boy! Leah named son number four Judah, meaning "praise."

"Now Rachel saw that she bore Jacob no children, she became jealous of her sister; and she said to Jacob, 'Give me children, or else I will die'" (Genesis 30:1).

Rachel was becoming a little uneasy at this point, and the jealousy was raging. She grew impatient and became upset with Jacob, blaming him for her infertility. Have we seen this before?

A woman's scorn is an ugly thing. Each of these sisters was filled with scorn for one another; it made Leah less attractive and took away from the natural beauty Rachel was apparently born with.

Read Genesis 30:2–16.

The level to which they were sinking was about to go lower. We see Rachel exchange intimate time with her husband for Leah's mandrakes. *"Bickering and shameless bargaining characterized this bigamous household"* (Genesis 30:14–18, NAS Ryrie Study Bible).

Leah informed Jacob that she had just *bought* time with him from her sister in exchange for her mandrakes. Jacob seemed to have little control in his own home. We don't see him assuming the role of the head of his home. We do not see him exercising authority over his wives or his home. Leah slept with him several more times and bore him two more sons and a daughter.

Read Genesis 30:17–24.

Leah and her maidservant birthed nine children for Jacob; Rachel and her maidservant birthed two. Basically, we see four sets of children.

"Then God remembered Rachel, and God gave heed to her and opened her womb." God remembered her and she gave birth to a son named Joseph. God was gracious to remember Rachel. We are never forgotten or abandoned by our heavenly Father.

Final score was Leah nine and Rachel three. Neither sister won. No one wins when envy, jealousy, and rivalry exists; everyone involved loses something!

What Rachel lost:

The genuine love and respect of her husband

Her relationship with her sister

The years envy and jealousy stole from her

What Leah lost:

The respect of her husband

Her relationship with her sister

The years envy and jealousy stole from her

The cost of sin is great! Rivalry, jealousy, and envy are sin. No sin is worth the price of your earthly relationships and certainly not worth the separation it causes between you and your heavenly Father. Sin is a loss, not a win!

"I have seen that every labor and every skill which is done is the result of rivalry between a man and his neighbor. This too is vanity and striving after the wind" (Ecclesiastes 4:4, NASB).

"Now the deeds of the flesh are evident, which are immorality, impurity, sensuality, idolatry, sorcery, enmities, strife, jealousy, outbursts of anger, disputes, dissensions, factions, envying, drunkenness, carousing, and things like these, of which I forewarned you, that those who practice such things will not inherit the kingdom of God" (Galatians 5:19–21, NASB).

Close in prayer.

Week Six Discussion Questions

Where did Jacob first see Rachel? *He saw her at a well upon his arrival in Haran.*

What was Rachel's title? *She was a shepherdess.*

Rachel ran off; where did she go? *She went to tell her father about Jacob.*

At the end of the month, what was the question Laban posed to Jacob? *"Should you therefore serve me for nothing? Tell me, what shall your wages be?" Why should he work for nothing? Laban was asking him what he felt his labor was worth.*

How are Laban's daughters, Rachel and Leah, described? *Leah had weak eyes. Rachel was beautiful of form and face. The people of that day placed great value on eyes that sparkled; Leah's eyes obviously lacked luster. Rachel had the more lovely eyes and overall beauty.*

It is obvious that Jacob loved Rachel from the very first time he saw her at the well. What deal did he make with Laban on behalf of obtaining Rachel for his wife? *"I will serve you seven years for your younger daughter Rachel." Laban agrees.*

If you were Leah, how do you think you would feel if your younger sister was chosen before you, and on top of that, the young man who had chosen your younger sister offered to give up seven years of his life for her! *I would imagine she was hurt, embarrassed, felt abandoned, was a little jealous of her sister. She must have felt she would never marry. She had to wonder who would ever find her beautiful.*

Jacob served his seven years and then what happened? *"So Jacob served seven years for Rachel and they seemed to him but a few days because of his love for her. Then Jacob said to Laban, 'Give me my wife, for my time is completed, that I may go into her.' Now it came about in the evening that he took his daughter Leah, and brought her to him; and Jacob went into her. So it came about in the morning that, behold, it was Leah! And he said to Laban, 'What is this you have done to me? Was it not for Rachel that I served you? Why then have you deceived me?'" Laban deceived him and gave him Leah instead of Rachel.*

How must Leah have felt knowing this? *She was probably angry, spiteful, and jealous of the love and attention he gave Rachel.*

What did Leah name her firstborn son? *Reuben, meaning "Look a son!"*

At this point, how do you think Rachel felt? *She felt she was losing two to zero.*

What other feelings might Rachel have had? *Envy, jealousy, spite, and rage toward Leah, impatience in waiting to get pregnant, and a willingness to exchange Jacob's love for a baby.*

After bearing Jacob three sons, did he love Leah? *No, he still loved Rachel more.*

Who did Jacob say was responsible? *"Am I in the place of God, who has withheld from you the fruit of the womb?" In other words, he said, "God has allowed this."*

Here we go again. Where have we seen a woman who could not wait on God and did exactly what Rachel is about to do? *Sarah, who gave Abraham her maidservant, Hagar.*

What was Rachel's solution to her problem of infertility? *She gave Jacob her maidservant, Bilhah.*

Did this solve Rachel's problems? *No, now she was jealous of Bilhah. She just increased her rival from one to two.*

What did Leah do after seeing that Rachel's maidservant had born two sons to Jacob? *Leah gave her maidservant, Zilpah, to Jacob since her womb was closed. She did not want to be outdone by her sister's maidservant. The score was Leah six, Rachel two!*

Who do you think won? *Neither girl won. They each lost something.*

Week 7

Baking Made Fun and Easy

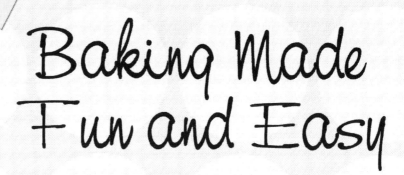

Week Seven: Baking Made Fun and Easy

Week Seven Lesson Plan

I. Leader opens in prayer

II. Devotional

Miriam—A Woman Filled with Jealousy. Read Exodus chapters 1 and 2, 15:20–21, and chapter 24 in order to prepare. (For help in preparing refer to lesson outline in Devotional section of Leader Guide.)

III. Time in the Kitchen

- Move to the kitchen.

- Review the importance of measuring correctly when baking. Measuring in cooking does not have to be as precise as it does in baking. Explain. (See Lesson Three on measurement to review.)

- Baking options for today's lesson: Choose one of the options below for today's Time in the Kitchen.

    1) *Snowflake Cookies.* Due to the fact the cookie dough has to be chilled, it is best to make ahead of time. Divide the young women into groups of three to four. In making the *Snowflake Cookies*, be sure they coat the cookie sheets; explain why. Have a large Ziploc® bag for each group in order to drop the rounded cookie dough into confectioners' sugar for coating dough. Bake according to recipe. Place on cooling rack once removed from oven. (A leader without a teaching assignment can be asked to watch over the cookies as you begin the lesson on Quick Mixes and/or Breads.)

    2) *Piecrust.* Using *Nancy's Piecrust* recipe, let each young woman make her own piecrust and place it in individual tin pie pans to take home (can be purchased at any dollar store). Have two piecrusts on hand; one prebaked and the other unbaked. Explain the difference between an unbaked, filled piecrust to be baked with filling and an empty piecrust that will be baked first, and then filled with a pudding filling. Divide young women into three groups, have two groups make two different fillings to go into prebaked pie shells (chocolate, coconut, or banana), and have the third group make the meringue. (See *Nancy's Meringue* recipe.) Chill pies and taste at the end of class. Explain: A fruit pie is filled with a fruit filling that is placed in an uncooked crust, and then baked following directions in recipe. A pudding-filled piecrust is one that is first pricked with a fork, baked until lightly browned, cooled, filled with pudding, topped with a meringue, and browned slightly in the oven or topped with whipped cream.

- While cookies are baking or you are waiting for pies to chill, discuss the Quick Mixes and go over recipes that can be made using Quick Mixes. Point out that homemade baking powder has fewer additives, is aluminum free, and much healthier. You also save money by making your own.

- If time allows, demonstrate how to *proof* yeast with ½ cup water and 1 tablespoon sugar. Explain why it is necessary in making different types of bread. Refer to yeast bread recipes. Have samples of a few different types of yeast breads.

- Have a variety of breads on hand—yeast bread, white or wheat, or yeast rolls. Fruit breads or some quick breads—poppy seed, strawberry, and zucchini. (Leadership can bring any variety of breads already baked and ready to taste.) Demonstrate how using a clear cellophane bag with a mini loaf of bread, tied with ribbon along with a scripture verse, can make a great gift, as well as an evangelistic tool. (Best price for cellophane bags is at Hobby Lobby® in the gift-wrap aisle).

- Taste pies and breads

IV. Week Seven Lesson Sheets

    INTRODUCTION: Girls' Day Out
    TEACHING NOTES: ALL ABOUT BREADS AND YEAST
    DEVOTIONAL: Miriam

V. Equipment for Week Seven

- For Cookies: Two prepared, chilled recipes of the *Snowflake Cookie* dough, cookie sheets, nonstick spray, plastic and metal spatulas, wood spoons, confectioners' sugar, and large Ziploc® bags

- For Pie: Tin pie pans (one for each participant). Ingredients for making *Nancy's Piecrust*. Bowls, measuring cups, spatulas, wire pastry blenders, forks, wooden spoons, rolling pins, extra flour/pastry mats, ingredients for two flavors of pie filling selected by leadership, ingredients to make meringue. See *Nancy's Meringue* recipe

- For proofing yeast, have 1-cup measuring cup, warm water, 1 tablespoon sugar, and a packet of dry-active yeast

- If time allows and baking mix is made, you will need ingredients called for in baking mix recipe and plastic zipper-lock bags for each young woman to take a sample home

- A variety of breads, a package of yeast, water, sugar to proof, bowl, and spoon. Cellophane bags, ribbon, and scripture cards to demo wrapping breads for gift giving

Introduction: Girls' Day Out

When you were a little girl, did you ever play house and pretend you were baking a cake? Did you ever have an Easy-Bake Oven? Oh, I did! Yes, on both accounts. However, I never found the Easy-Bake Oven to be easy, only messy! Did you ever notice how awful the Easy-Bake cake tasted? It was absolutely nothing like the cakes my mom used to make. I am glad I didn't base my baking ability on my failures with my Easy-Bake Oven! Being a female, you know how much little girls like to play and pretend they are mommies, taking care of their baby dolls, cleaning and baking cakes, just enjoying every part of their pretend play, without a care in the world.

When I was around seven, I spent the summer with my grandparents. While there, I discovered a treasure under the basement stairwell. It was a wicker picnic basket, complete with plates, napkins, cups, forks, spoons, and a sweet little tablecloth. I spent hours playing with that basket and pretending to make all kinds of wonderful food for my pretend family. We would have cake, ice cream, cookies, and cupcakes. Nothing healthy, of course! The fun part of pretend play is that you can bake anything your little heart desires and eat as much as you want. Oh, the hours of fun I had playing with that basket!

I now have four granddaughters from age ten down to one year. I have noticed something about little girls: not only do they love to pretend in their little play kitchen, they love to be in the kitchen with Mommy or Mimi. The oldest, Annalise, and I have begun to have a *Girls' Day Out* every two or three months. Every time I ask her what she wants to do, she answers, "Go to your house and bake." She loves to measure, pour, and break the eggs. One time, we bought an ironing board and iron, a play one, of course. We came back to the house and put on our aprons. She ironed her doll clothes while I got everything ready to bake. We had such a good time in the kitchen together. The cookies were so good hot out of the oven. Pop really enjoys our *Girls' Day Out*. His favorite thing is a hot cookie right out of the oven; what man wouldn't? That day, Annalise and I were making a special memory. She loved being in the kitchen with Mimi. It might be the last time she will ever enjoy ironing, though!

Teaching Notes: All about Breads and Yeast[18]

Breads

Do you find it overwhelming to even begin the process of making bread? Success in bread making occurs when you are well informed about the ingredients involved in the bread-making process. Once you understand, you are ready for success. When making breads, most recipes call for bread flour; use unbleached white bread flour. The benefit of bread flour in a recipe is that it is high in protein content, which leads to gluten development—structure—in bread. Some recipes will call for all-purpose combined with bread flour. With any bread recipe, begin with using half of the flour called for and increase it as the dough is mixed. You may find, you need a little more or even a little less. The weather, the flour, and your handling of the dough will determine how much you will need. It is best to go with texture of dough in bread making, over the measurement called for; this will help in determining just how much flour you need. In the process of mixing and kneading the dough, start with mixing the yeast and water together, and then add other ingredients and most of the flour called for in the recipe. Once the dough becomes heavier, attach a dough hook to your stand mixer[8*] to knead, or remove from bowl and knead by hand. Kneading is an over-and-fold motion using the heels of your hand or a dough hook. Do not overwork the dough; just slowly maneuver the dough in a repeated motion. Dough should become a resilient mass with elasticity to it. When the dough gets to this point, it is ready to rise; just follow recipe and enjoy your success!

Yeast

When yeast is mixed with flour and water, it feeds off the sugars present in the flour-water combination. In that fusion, it creates a carbon dioxide gas, which leavens (rises) the bread. Once the dough is baked, the taste of the gas is gone, but the structural transformation remains. This process is similar to a helium balloon: the helium disappears, but mysteriously, you are left with the balloon structure. In using dry yeast, you have the choice of instant or active dry yeast as well as fresh yeast. Most recipes call for active dry yeast, but if you prefer rapid-rise yeast, you can use it with no change to your recipe. Rapid rise is valued for its heartiness and consistent performance; it speeds up the process of bread making. With dry yeast or fresh yeast, you can expect a 15 to 30 percent longer rise time. Red Star Yeast or Fleischman's Yeast is the most commonly available yeast brands. Rapid rise yeast is good for all baking and is especially good for sweet bread recipes. It can be mixed with flour, according to the package directions. For best results, mix yeast with the amount of water (should be 100°F to 110°F) called for in the recipe. Mixing all types of yeast with the water hydrates the yeast. When this is done, there is no need to wait for the rapid-rise to proof, as is the case with dry yeast. Once yeast is opened, it must be refrigerated. Pay close attention to the expiration date on the package of yeast. It is best if used within the dates given.

---

[18] Marcy Goldman, *A Passion for Baking* (Oxmoor House, 2007).

WEEK SEVEN: Miriam—A Woman Filled with Jealousy

Biblical History—Read Exodus chapters 1–2. In these chapters, we see the children of Israel are enslaved in Egypt under Pharaoh, the king of Egypt. The name *Pharaoh* means "great house" and is a title for the king, not his actual name. Pharaoh, who is in office at this time, was threatened by the size of the Israelite people and decided to whittle them down to a size he could manage. He said to his people, *"Behold, the people of the sons of Israel are more and mightier than we. Come let us deal wisely with them, or else they will multiply and in the event of war they will also join themselves to those who hate us, and fight against us and depart from the land."*

First, Pharaoh placed taskmasters over them to afflict them with hard labor. But what he did not count on was God's hand upon the children of Israel—the more the Egyptians abused them the greater their numbers grew. Their lives were made bitter by the Egyptians; abuse and torture were prevalent. Pharaoh then decided that hard labor and abuse were not working, so he called in the midwives and told them, *"When you are helping the Hebrew women to give birth and see them upon the birthstool, if it is a son, then you shall put him to death; but if it is a daughter, they shall live."*

Praise the Lord! The midwives feared God more than Pharaoh. *"But the midwives feared God, and did not do as the King of Egypt had commanded them, but let the boys live."* They informed the king they could not help but let the babies live because the Hebrew women were very vigorous and gave birth before they were able to arrive to deliver the baby. God was good to the midwives because they chose right over wrong; obedience equals blessings.

Out of frustration and anger, Pharaoh told all the Israelites that every male baby born to them was to be thrown into the Nile River, but the female babies would be allowed to live. Now Miriam came on the scene. Jochebed, the mother of Moses, and her daughter, Miriam, devised a plan to save their little male baby named Moses. Jochebed constructed a basket of reeds and placed him in it. Miriam slipped down through the reeds at the edge of the Nile just about the time Pharaoh's daughter and all her servants came down to the river's edge to bathe. She strategically placed the basket with baby Moses inside the water and said a prayer, giving it a gentle shove in the direction of Pharaoh's daughter. *"And she saw the basket among the reeds and sent her maid, and she brought it to her. When she opened it she saw the child, and behold, the boy was crying. And she had pity on him and said, "This is one of the Hebrew's children."*

Now it was time for Miriam to appear on the stage and play her part. She popped up from the edge of the reeds and said, *"Shall I go and call a nurse for you from the Hebrew women that she may nurse the child for you?"* Pharaoh's daughter said to her, *"Go ahead."* So Jochebed, the mother willing to give up her son in order to save his life, got him back. She was paid to nurse him until he was weaned at the age of three, and then He was taken into the royal household at that point.

Let's fast forward to Exodus 15:1–18 where we see the celebration that followed God's deliverance of His children from the Egyptians. He dried up the Red Sea, they walked across, and their feet were not even muddy. As the Egyptians stepped foot into the sea, Pharaoh and all his men were swallowed up, horses, chariots, and all. In these verses, we see Moses having written a beautiful song of celebration, expressing gratefulness to the Lord for His deliverance on behalf of the children of Israel as well as the destruction of Pharaoh and his army.

To discover the rest of their deliverance story, read Exodus 15:20–21 and chapter 24.

For additional reference, read Exodus 15:22–24.

Read Numbers chapters 11 and 12.

*"Then Miriam and Aaron **spoke against** Moses because of the Cushite woman whom he married; and they said, 'Has the Lord indeed spoken only through Moses? Has he not spoken through us as well?'"*

"Spoke against" is a feminine verb meaning Miriam *led* the criticism. When we lead out in criticism against those in authority over us, we can wrongly influence those around us, as Miriam did.

Donna Gaines, noted author and Bible teacher, says, "A complaining spirit always leads to a critical spirit."

Miriam started with *jealousy*, then moved to *complaining* and ended with a *critical spirit*.

Perhaps her thoughts were something like: *Moses is not doing a good job leading. I could do a better job running these people and do it more efficiently than he does. Is he the only one God can speak through? I don't think so! Why should Moses be the leader of our people? He can't even make a wise choice in selecting a wife. We need to vote him out. I am the woman for the people of Israel.*

In the hypothetical statement above, we see jealousy, then a complaining spirit, followed by a critical spirit.

Numbers 12:2b is a very convicting verse: *"And the Lord heard it."*

God hears our every word. If we truly believed that, we would be much more careful of our conversations. He also says we will be judged by our every word. Wow!

What happened next got their attention, I am sure of it! *"Suddenly* (out of nowhere) *the Lord said to Moses and Aaron and to Miriam, "You* **three** *come out to the tent of meeting."*

Dianne's Personal Testimony: (Leadership should feel free to share their own experiences.)

I was the middle of four children. When we fought with one another, my dad called us out by name. I can hear him now. "Dianne Lynn!" When he used the first and middle name, I knew I was in trouble! Just in case he happened to be punishing the innocent one, he called out all who were involved in the altercation and exercised equal opportunity punishment. As a child, my dad and mom always had a tone of voice that let me know without a shadow of a doubt I was in BIG trouble!

God called all three of them. Can you imagine hearing God's voice thundering from heaven calling out your name? I wonder if they knew by the tone of His voice that they were in *BIG* trouble.

"So the three of them came out." I'll bet they did! They must have known there was no hiding from God. He hears, He sees, and He holds us accountable.

Dianne's Personal Testimony: *I can remember once, when I was little, my dad had warned me over and over again, "Do not run in the church building." But I failed to heed the warning one Sunday night and got caught. Once home, Dad told me to go down to my room, put on my pajamas, and he would be right down with his belt; punishment was on the way!* God was coming down with his belt to punish Miriam and Aaron.

"Then the Lord came down in a pillar of cloud and stood at the doorway of the tent, and he called Miriam and Aaron."

In essence, God said, "As for the prophets among you, I make myself known to them in visions, not so with my beloved Moses. With him, I SPEAK FACE TO FACE." In other words, God spoke to Moses directly!

The verses tell us that after God said what He came to say, He departed. Once again, sin separates us from God.

I have a friend who calls the punishment God inflicted upon Miriam as, "God's time out."

"So Miriam was shut up outside the camp for seven days, and the people did not move on until Miriam was received again."

God forgave and restored Miriam. The NAS Ryrie Study Bible says, *"Had God not forgiven Miriam, she would have been an outcast."*

What do we learn from Miriam?

- Jealousy is an unattractive outfit on a woman.
- Sin is progressive. Miriam started with jealousy, moved to complaining, and ended with a critical spirit.
- Never challenge God's anointed.
- God sees the motive of the heart.
- God hates pride.
- Never speak out against God's anointed.
- God hears our every word, and we will be accountable for each one of them.
- There is always a price to pay for sin.
- A public sin calls for public punishment; all the camp witnessed her punishment.
- God is waiting with abundant mercy and grace to forgive us of our sins and restore us to a right relationship with Him.

Psalm 32:1, NASB, says, *"How blessed is he whose transgression is forgiven, whose sin is covered."*

1 Corinthians 13:4, NASB, says, *"Love is patient, love is kind and is not jealous; love does not brag and is not arrogant."*

Close in prayer.

Week Seven Discussion Questions

- How do the verses read today describe Miriam? *She is the prophetess and Aaron's sister, which means she was Moses' sister. She was obviously gifted musically and a leader of women.*

- What did the Lord hear? *Miriam and Aaron complaining and criticizing God's chosen leader. There was jealousy and judgment in their words. God hears our every word and we will be accountable for each one.*

- What does the verse in Numbers 12:3 tell us about Moses? *"Now the man Moses was very humble, more than any man on the face of the earth."*

- Why do you think God put this verse here? *In order to draw a contrast between Miriam, Aaron, and His called leader, Moses. Miriam and Aaron were anything but humble!*

- God called their names and they stepped forward. What is the significance of their stepping forward? *In stepping forward, they were acknowledging their guilt.*

- Once the cloud disappeared, what happened to Miriam? *She was leprous. The verse says, "She was white as snow."*

- What did Aaron do at this point? *He confessed and begged for mercy on Miriam's behalf. He basically was saying, "We really didn't mean it, Moses."*

- What does Moses do? *"Moses cried out to the Lord, saying, 'O God, heal her, I pray.'" He interceded on her behalf—a sign of Moses' forgiveness toward Miriam.*

- Did God instantly answer Moses' prayer on behalf of Miriam? *No!*

- Why not? *Sin has a price. The price Miriam paid was separation from her people. "If a father had spit in her face, would she not bear her shame for seven days? Let her be shut up for seven days outside the camp, and afterward she may be received again."*

Questions to Ponder

Has there ever been a time when you were jealous of someone in authority or led out in criticizing them? Were you sorry to have ever been a part of such a thing?

Were you convicted about your behavior? Did you go and apologize to the person you had criticized?

Week 8
It's a Chinet Evening

Week Eight: It's a Chinet Evening—Hospitality Made Easy

Week Eight Lesson Plan

I. Leader opens in prayer

II. Devotional

Rachel—A Woman of Great Faith. Read Joshua chapter 1 and 2 to prepare. (For help in preparing refer to lesson outline in Devotional Section of Leader Guide.)

III. Lesson

- Today's lesson is on hospitality. The definition of *hospitable* is "to treat guest with warmth and generosity." Romans 12:13 says, "*Share with God's people who are in need. Practice hospitality.*"

  The Message Bible says, "*Help needy Christians; be inventive in hospitality.*" 1 Peter 4:9–10 says, "*Be hospitable to one another without complaint. As each one has received a special gift, employ it in serving one another as good stewards of the manifold grace of God.*" Talk to the young women about the importance of opening their homes to others; it is a biblical principle. It doesn't matter if we have little or much, if we can cook, or how small our home, we are all to minister to others through hospitality. Other verses on hospitality: Romans 12:9–13 and Hebrews 13:2. Emphasize keeping it *simple*! (Refer to *Helpful Hints on Hospitality*.)

- Refer to the *Fun Ice Breakers* sheet. Young women can use these sheets when hosting a dinner party.

- Refer to the *Hospitality Made Fun and Affordable* sheet. (Note: the class will prepare one of the menus for their *Time in the Kitchen* today.)

- Teach the importance of proper place settings. Read Scenario #1 or Scenario #2. Discuss the importance of being educated in the area of proper etiquette. Knowing what to expect in social settings can make us more comfortable in circumstances such as those described in the scenarios read today.

  Fill large one-gallon Ziploc® bags with appropriate paper and plastic dinnerware to make a casual place setting. *For Example*: Dinner plate, salad/bread plate, water glass, tea glass or coffee cup, knife, spoon, salad fork, and dinner fork; label each piece. Divide young women into three to four groups, each group receiving a bag. Using the kitchen and dining room table, allow ten minutes for each group to position their place setting. When they are finished, have the leadership go around and check their work. If needed, kindly correct any mistakes. Explain the importance of knowing what pieces go where on a table and their proper usage. **Read scenario #1:** *Your in-laws call and inform you that they want to take the entire family to a five-star restaurant to celebrate their anniversary. You have never been to such a nice restaurant before. What will you do with the third fork on your left or the spoons placed at the top of your dinner plate?* **Scenario #2**: *You have only been on the new job a week. Your boss invites you to dinner, along with his wife and two other co-workers. He tells you to meet them Friday night at 6:30 at his private country club. You arrive at 6:25! As you are seated, you look down at the dinner table to see numerous pieces of* *silverware along with a variety of small plates and glasses. You are panicked. What piece are you going to use first?* Discuss the importance of being educated about such things and how knowing what to expect can help us be more comfortable in the circumstances described above.

- Proper Serving Rules. During your *Time in the Kitchen*, while each young woman is enjoying her $1 *gourmet* pizza and the appetizers supplied by the leadership, demonstrate proper serving rules by role playing. Have two leaders, one seated at the kitchen or dining room table and one serving, demonstrate the proper etiquette for passing food and the proper way a host or hostess serves their seated guests. Demonstrate the correct way to serve your seated guests their dinner plate and then remove it. Also demonstrate from which side to serve drinks and then refill or remove the glasses. Illustrate the correct direction to pass food when the entire party of guests is seated. Go over the rules for serving a buffet.

IV. Time in the Kitchen

- Choose one of the *Hospitality Made Fun and Affordable* menus and have the young women prepare it during your *Time in the Kitchen*. Have all necessary ingredients. If choosing the $1 *Pizza Made Edible* recipe, supply one $1 pizza for every group of three to four girls and all the sides to make a plain cheese pizza into a gourmet pizza. Divide the young women into groups of three to four and have them prepare their pizza. The $1 *Pizza Made Edible* is fast and easy and does not require much baking time. Once the preparation is complete, have the class taste their creation.

- Discuss the fun potlucks the young women have either hosted or participated in. Leadership may want to bring a few of their favorite appetizer recipes, already prepared, to share with the class. As the young women enjoy the food, demonstrate the proper serving rules. See today's Lesson Plan section.

- If time allows, you can begin today's lesson with using the Fun Ice Breakers sheet to illustrate getting a conversation started when entertaining guests, or play a game from the Helpful Hints on Hospitality sheet..

- Answer any questions

V. Week Eight Lesson Sheets

INTRODUCTION: An Example to Follow
DEVOTIONAL: Rahab

VI. Equipment for Week Eight

- One large gallon Ziploc® bag for each group, filled with pieces for casual place settings, with a marker identifying each piece. *For Example*: Items marked: dinner plate, salad plate, bread plate, dinner fork, salad fork, tea spoon, etc. to be used to teach place settings

- Ingredients for preparing one menu idea on the *Hospitality Made Fun and Affordable* sheet. Paper plates, forks, and napkins. Hostess provides drinks. <u>Optional</u>: Appetizers prepared and brought by leadership

Introduction Week Eight: An Example to Follow

I mentioned previously that I grew up in a modest home. We had very few of what you might call fancy or elegant possessions, especially in the area of entertaining. Yet, our home was always open to anyone and everyone. It didn't matter the color of your skin, your background, or your economic status, you were always welcome! My dad was a college professor. Over the years, my mom taught young people from junior high up to the college level. So students were always welcome in our home. Mom and Dad are both very personable, and folks have always been drawn to them. Their hearts are bigger than they are!

My parents eloped and married when Dad was twenty and Mom was seventeen. They didn't have a wedding registry! There were no wedding showers and no beautiful wedding gifts, as we often see today. I do believe they had one wedding shower, once they arrived home. You did not find twelve-piece place settings of Wedgewood China or the latest pottery pattern in our home. There was no Arthur Court and certainly no sterling silver flatware. Yet, none of this mattered. I don't think anyone who came to our home left there saying, "Can you believe she did not even have a twelve-piece place setting of her everyday dishes?" Instead, they went away feeling loved, cared for, having laughed a lot, and with memories of a good time in our home.

Why is it that in our "keeping up with the Joneses" society we let the *things* we *do not have* keep us from using what we *do have* to minister and bless others? The prevailing attitude today is that we have to possess certain things before we can invite others into our home. Where did this attitude come from? When that is your attitude, you miss out on relationships that could have blessed, challenged, and enriched your life. I have heard young women say, "I don't set a beautiful table like Angela," or "I can't cook like Kelly." Who cares! Who says you're supposed to be like Angela or Kelly anyway? If my parents had had that attitude or those thoughts, I would have missed out on so much. I wouldn't have the fond memories of fun times with so many special people. I still remember sitting on the floor in our living room while the preacher sat in the *only chair*. It was nestled in the corner of the room near the opening to the kitchen. He told us story after story, and the three of us kids just laughed and laughed as he entertained us. What if my parents had said, "Our house is too small and too sparsely furnished to have the guest preacher stay with us?" What if my mom had said she couldn't have the guest preacher because she couldn't cook like Mrs. Smith?

I am grateful my parents were willing to open our home and be hospitable to anyone and everyone who entered there. How interesting that my siblings and I love to invite people into our homes. All four of us desire to be hospitable to others. We now have the joy of seeing our children desiring to do the same. My parents set the example for me; now my girls are setting an example for their children. Oh, what fond memories my grandchildren will have!

WEEK EIGHT: Rahab—A Woman of Great Faith

Read Joshua chapters 1 and 2.

Biblical History—The author of this book is Joshua. There are some parts of the book believed to be inserted by Eliezer the priest or by his son, Phineas. Joshua was born in Egypt and his name means "Yahweh is salvation." Before Moses' death, he was commissioned as his successor. Moses was not allowed to lead the people into Palestine because of his unbelief in striking the rock for water. Joshua led the people in their conquest of Canaan, the Promised Land. The qualities he was known for were his faith, obedience, courage, and his devotion to the word of God. The book describes the conquest and division of the land of Canaan. The land was filled with corruption, brutal religious practices, and idolatry. The children of Israel were instructed by God to completely destroy the Canaanites, but because they did not, their religion (the Canaanite's) was tolerated and frequently absorbed into the Israelite community. The book begins with God's commissioning Joshua and the entrance into the land of Canaan. The main emphasis in the book is the faithfulness of God, the importance of the written law, and the holiness of God in judging the sins of the Canaanites. (NAS Ryrie Study Bible).

Read Joshua 2:1–6.

In chapter 2, an unlikely person came on the scene to be used of God; her name was Rahab.

The king was told that there were spies from Israel in the city lodging at Rahab's home. These men were sent by Joshua to search out the land.

Rahab must have been seeking after God, because she recognized the two men of God.

A friend of mine has said in relationship to Rahab, "God always reveals Himself to anyone seeking after Him." God knew she was seeking Him.

We see the chief sending word to Rahab, *"Bring out the men who have come to you, who have entered your house, for they have come to search out all the land."*

In chapter 2:7–14, we see Rahab's house was apparently on the western wall (toward the mountains) and she sent the chief's men in the opposite direction. Meanwhile, the spies were on her roof.

Before the two spies retired for the night, she went up to them and in verse 8–9, we see a beautiful statement of faith, *"Now before they lay down she came up to them on the roof and said to the men, 'I know that the Lord has given you the land, and that the terror of you has fallen on us, and that all the inhabitants of the land have melted away before you. For we have heard how the Lord dried up the water of the Red Sea before you when you came out of Egypt, and what you did to the two kings of the Amorites who were beyond the Jordan, to Sihon and Og, whom you utterly destroyed. When we heard it, our hearts melted and no courage remained in any man any longer because of you; for the Lord your God, He is God in heaven above and on the earth beneath'"* (NASB).

Read Joshua 2:15–24. Rahab lowered a rope and let them out through a window and down the city wall. She instructed them to go to the hill country and stay there three days until the chief's men gave up looking for them.

We see her agreeing to what they had instructed her to do. She sent them on their way and immediately tied a scarlet thread in the window.

Rahab did not waste any time getting the scarlet thread on the window. We see her belief (faith) in the coming of Israel with their God; the God of heaven was coming to destroy the city. We see her immediate obedience.

Rahab didn't take any chances; that cord was probably hung before the two spies were out of sight!

Don't you know Rahab immediately went about gathering her family into her house, not knowing when the Israelites would be coming? I would imagine everyone who passed by, she invited in, but many did not believe her when she said that the God of Israel and His people were coming to take the land and destroy the city. (Although they had heard of Israel and the Living God for the past forty years.)

It must have been a lot like Noah in the Ark. No one believed him, but the rain came! And the spies would return with all of Israel.

In Joshua 6:20–27, we see that God is faithful. He always keeps His Word, and He is willing to save anyone who will put his or her full trust in Him.

In Luke 7:48–49, Jesus was most likely speaking to a prostitute, though her identity is somewhat uncertain. This woman took an expensive vile of perfume and anointed His feet. *"Then He said to her, 'Your sins have been forgiven'"* (NASB).

In reading Matthew 1:5, we see Rahab mentioned in the genealogy of Christ; she is referred to as a harlot. There was no sugar coating it! God called her what she was, showing us what Rahab was saved from.

Fast forward to Hebrews 11:31, NASB, and read aloud: *"By faith Rahab the harlot did not perish along with those who were disobedient, after she had welcomed the spies in peace."*

Rahab was listed in the Faith Hall of Fame. Wow! She set the example for each of us when it comes to having a dynamic faith.

What qualified Rahab for the Faith Hall of Fame?

- She *acknowledged* God as the God of heaven.
- She *believed in* Him.
- She *trusted* Him.
- She *obeyed* Him.
- She *exercised* great faith in waiting for Him to come and save her along with her household.
- Webster's Dictionary defines *faith* as, "a belief or trust in God." Rahab had faith; she qualified!

Have you acknowledged God as the God of heaven and the Lord of your life?

How is your belief? Do you really believe that no matter *what you have done* and no matter *what you are* that God *can* and *will* save you?

How is your trust?

Do you trust God to save you, to keep you, and to be there whenever you need Him?

Do you trust Him with your life, your husband, your children, your present, and your future?

How is your faith?

Do you have faith to believe that He can and will save those who come to Him?

Rahab the harlot, Faith Hall of Fame Inductee—a woman with a past, but oh, the future she had to look forward to when she bowed before the God of heaven with a grateful heart!

Close in prayer.

Week Eight Discussion Questions

- Why did Joshua only send out two spies? Why did he keep their mission a secret? *Joshua learned an important lesson at Kadesh-barnea and kept the spy mission quiet from the Israelites so that if an unfavorable report was brought back, the people would not be discouraged. (Refer back to Numbers 13–14.)*

- What was Rahab's occupation? *She was a well-known prostitute in Jericho.*

- What is Rahab's response to the spies? *First, she hid them. Then she sent word to the chief saying, yes, they had come to her but she was unaware of what country they were from. She told him that they left by the gate and she did not know where they had gone. Rahab told the chief's men that they needed to pursue these two Israelite men quickly and catch them.*

- Was it okay for Rahab to lie when the Bible clearly says, "You shall not lie?" *The NAS Ryrie Study Bible says, "Rahab's actions, though not in line with the spiritual prohibition against lying, were evidence that she believed the God of Israel was the true God. The Bible commends her faith, not her lying. (See Hebrews 11:31 and James 2:25.) God's grace is remarkably demonstrated in giving her faith, sparing her life, and including her in the messianic line.*

- Where were the spies hidden? *"But she had brought them up to the roof and hidden them in the stocks of flax which she had laid in order on the roof.*

- When speaking to the spies, what does Rahab's statement sound like to you? *It sounds like a profession of faith. She acknowledged God as the God of heaven.*

- What did she ask of the two spies for providing shelter and protection for them? *"Now, therefore, please swear to me by the Lord, since I have dealt kindly with you, that you also will deal kindly with my father's household, and give me a pledge of truth, and spare my father, and my mother and my brothers and my sisters, with all who belong to them, deliver our lives from death." She requested protection for her and all her household.*

- What was their response? *"So, the men said to her, 'Our life for yours if you do not tell this business of ours; and it shall come about when the Lord gives us the land that we will deal kindly and faithfully with you.'" They would watch out for her and her household when they returned to take the city.*

- What did the spies instruct her to do prior to their next visit? *"Unless, when we come into the land, you tie a scarlet thread in the window through which you let us down, and gather to yourself into the house your father and your mother and your brother's and all your father's household. It shall come about that anyone who goes out of the doors of your house into the street, his blood shall be on his head, and we shall be free; but anyone who is with you in the house, his blood shall be on our head if a hand is laid on him. But, if you tell this business of ours, then we shall be free from the oath which you have made us swear." She is to gather all her household and keep them inside the walls for protection, place a scarlet thread in her window, and wait. They would keep safe all who were within her walls.*

- What was the significance of the scarlet thread? *(See Exodus 12:7–13.) The sacrificial blood placed on the doorpost and God passing over. The scarlet thread was a picture of the shed blood of Christ, which was to come, the blood that covers over our sins.*

- When the walls of Jericho fell, what happened to Rahab and her household? *"Joshua said to the two men who had spied out the land, 'Go into the harlot's house and bring the woman and all she has out there, as you have sworn to her.' So the young men who were spies went in and brought out Rahab and her father and her mother and her brothers and all she had; they also brought out all her relatives and placed them outside the camp of Israel. They burned the city with fire, and all that was in it. However, Rahab the harlot and her father's household and all she had, Joshua spared; and she lived in the midst of Israel to this day, for she hid the messengers whom Joshua sent to spy on Jericho." She and her household were spared; the part of the wall where Rahab lived did not collapse. She and all those with her were placed in the camp of the Israelites.*

- What does this tell you about God? *He saves us in spite of our sin, and He never remembers our sins or our past.*

Week Nine Lesson: Date Night

A Couple's Night Out—Dinner and Dessert

This night is set aside for the young women and their husbands to have a *Date Night*. The leadership will prepare, and along with their spouses, will serve the meal to the young couples. The leadership has the option of serving buffet style or having a seated dinner; it will depend on the size of the hostess's home.

When the young couples arrive, serve an appetizer, and a hot or cold beverage. Let them mingle with one another, as well as with the leadership and their spouses. Once everyone has arrived, gather together and pray for the meal and your time together. Have the couples take their seats and serve dinner. If serving a seated dinner, have a few index cards on each table with questions written down for them to answer during dinner. This will encourage conversation, especially for those who didn't know one another prior to arriving. At each table, appoint a host couple to take responsibility for the cards (For sample questions see the *Ideas for Getting Acquainted* and the *Fun Ice Breakers* sheets in Week Eight.)

Once dinner is finished, serve dessert and coffee. Have everyone gather in a den or living room. The hostess and her husband, or the leader, will greet the couples. Have each couple introduce themselves and tell how they met along with a little something about themselves. For the sake of the husbands attending, explain the purpose of the Secrets study. Ask the group of husbands how their wives participating in the class has impacted their homes; wait for responses. Hostess or leader will ask each table group about the questions discussed at their table; this will encourage conversation among the group. If serving buffet style, the questions can be used during the gathering time. Thank them for coming and close out the evening. Leadership may want to plan a program for the evening. Be creative.

Week Nine Lesson Sheets

    INTRODUCTION: A Kiss or a Handshake
    MARRIAGE BOOK LIST

Introduction: A Kiss or a Handshake

The first date Mark and I had was attending a Christian concert on campus. I was so excited after his call. My mind filled with questions, such as what was I going to wear? I wanted to make a good impression; after all, he was a junior in college and here I was just a sophomore in high school. This was a big deal! I thought long and hard about my outfit and how I was going to wear my hair. The big night came and with it lots of butterflies, all flying in a circular formation in my stomach. I had only dated one other young man, so my experience with dating was limited, especially when it came to *college* guys!

Mark arrived looking very handsome; *fine* would be a better word. I had observed him from a distance for several months, and he was always nicely dressed. His shoes were freshly polished, and he was wearing the latest fashion. We went out to dinner and on to the concert. It was a fun evening; we found that we had a lot to talk about. Once we arrived to my house, I invited him in, but he politely declined. With a warm handshake, the evening was over. The next day, he called and we talked for a long time. In the weeks to follow, we had several dates, all ending in a polite, warm handshake followed by, *"Dianne, I really had a good time tonight."* Now, I was young and inexperienced at dating, but I thought a kiss meant he had a good time. What did a warm handshake mean? I was a little confused!

After a few months, it came—the *kiss*! I had to ask what I'd wanted to ask him for weeks: "Why did you wait so long?" He explained that he and a friend had agreed that neither of them would kiss a girl after a certain number of dates, just to see what she would do. They challenged each other as to whether or not the young woman would hang around. They called it, "The Florida Challenge"—both being from South Florida. I guess you have to be a guy to understand that one! We can all look back on our dating years; for some, it hasn't been very long ago and for others it has been quite some time. Why is dating a *priority* before we marry and not a *priority* afterwards? Perhaps, it's because before we marry, the guy is trying to *catch* the girl and of course, she wants to be *caught*. What about now that you're married? It would seem that the longer a couple is married the less they make dating a priority. After all, he's got her now!

As the years go by, there are careers to consider, the purchase of a first home, children being born, career changes, and then the purchase of the second home—bigger than the first—requiring additional bills and extra responsibility. The cost of a baby sitter is far more than you can afford, the finances are tight, and on and on. Perhaps there are many reasons or *excuses* for not *dating* your spouse, but spending time alone with your spouse is necessary for keeping the oneness in your relationship. A date night can spark communication (uninterrupted communication!) and cause you both to remember what drew you to one another in the first place. We, as your Secrets leadership, want to give you this date night in hopes that it will be a reminder to you and your spouse of how important it is to make date nights a priority in your marriage relationship. Enjoy!

Marriage Book List:

Love and War by John Eldredge and Stasi Eldredge

Sacred Marriage by Gary Thomas

The 8 Love Languages by Gary Chapman

Every Man's Marriage by Stephen Arterburn and Fred Stocker

Created to Be His Help Meet by Debi Pearl

Hidden Keys of a Loving and Lasting Marriage by Gary Smalley

Romantic Lovers by David and Carol Hocking

Intended for Pleasure by Ed Wheat, M.D. and Kaye Wheat

The Act of Marriage by Tim and Beverly LaHaye

Quiet Times for Couples by H. Norm Wright

The Love Dare by Stephen Kendrick

His Needs—Her Needs by Willard F. Harley

Have a New Husband by Friday by Dr. Kevin Leman

Love and Respect for a Lifetime by Dr. Emerson Eggerichs

Sheet Music by Dr. Kevin Leman

The Excellent Wife by Martha Pierce

Night Light by Dr. James and Shirley Dobson

Boundaries in Marriage by Dr. Henry Cloud and Dr. John Townsend

What's It Like to Be Married to Me? by Linda Dillow

Pray Big for Your Marriage by Will Davis Jr.

Intimacy Ignited by Linda Dillow

Intimate Issues by Linda Dillow

Momentary Marriage by John Piper

As Long as We Both Shall Live by Gary Smalley and Ted Cunningham

Young and in Love by Ted Cunningham

The Four Seasons of Marriage: Secrets to a Lasting Marriage by Gary Chapman

Girls Night Out
Dinner and Dessert for College and Single Women

As young women are arriving for the evening, serve appetizers and a beverage. After everyone has arrived, seat the young women and serve dinner. At each table, place an index card with questions that will spur conversation. Assign one young lady per table to oversee the questions. <u>Note</u>: For ideas, see *Ideas for Getting Acquainted* and *the Fun Ice Breakers* handout sheets for questions. Once dinner is complete, have the young women move to the living room; serve dessert and coffee. You may plan a game to be played, have a question and answer time between the young women and the leadership, or plan a creative craft idea. For craft ideas, see Pinterest.com.

Game Idea: Have the young women take a handful of M&Ms out of a bowl. Then inform them that for every M&M they took, they will have to tell something about themselves that no one else knows.

Week Nine Lesson Sheets

    INTRODUCTION A Kiss and a Handshake
    BOOKS FOR HER
    FOR YOUNG COLLEGE/SINGLE WOMEN
    TESTIMONY OF A YOUNG WOMAN WHO WAS WILLING TO WAIT by Leslie Hollowell
    FUN GIRL TIMES

Books for Her

One Thousand Gifts by Ann Voscamp

So Long Insecurity by Beth Moore

Kisses from Katie by Katie Davis

Lies Young Women Believe by Nancy Leigh DeMoss

Made to Crave for Young Women: Satisfying Your Deepest Desires with God by Lysa TerKeurst

Every Young Woman's Battle: Guarding Your Mind by Shannon Ethridge and Stephen Arterburn

A Young Woman After God's Own Heart by Elizabeth George

A Young Woman's Guide to Making Right Decisions by Elizabeth George

A Young Woman's Walk with God: Growing More Like Jesus by Elizabeth George

Courtesy and Kindness for Young Ladies by Emilie Barnes

Grace for the Good Girl by Emily P. Freeman

Unglued by Lysa TerKeurst

For Young College/Single Women

Tonight is a special night in which your leadership wants to honor you with dinner and dessert. The story on page 197, of how Mark and I began our dating years, is one that I hope you enjoyed reading. I have found that God works uniquely different in the lives of all His children. For me, God gave me my mate for life at a young age. I am grateful for many reasons, but mainly because Mark was diagnosed five years ago with a rare condition that has drastically changed our lives and our marriage. I am grateful that we were able to begin our relationship at such a young age and have the years we had before Mark became ill. Perhaps you are in high school, college, or single. No matter where you are, you can rest in knowing that God knows the mate He has chosen for you and in the right time, He will bring your lives together. His plans, His ways, and His timing are always perfect. So, relax and trust Him. I was blessed to find my mate at a young age, but I know of numerous young women who were willing to wait and God gave them a wonderful mate in which to share their lives. Waiting on God brings about the best for your life; do not settle for anything but God's best!

The testimony of a young woman who was willing to wait . . .

Many Are the Plans

I came to an understanding years ago, that *"Many are the plans in a man's heart, but it's the Lord's purpose that prevails"* (Proverbs 19:21).

I began at the early age of eight striving to determine the plans for my life. At this point, I was determined to be a detective and take my place as the fourth angel on *Charlie's Angels*. By age twelve, I was going to be a news anchorwoman. I sat for hours in the bathroom with my round brush, practicing my "and now for our local weather" voice.

Next up were my high school years. It was in that season of life that I realized I had a flare for teaching. My former third-grade teacher permitted me to "teach" a few lessons every week for a short period of time when I was her teacher's aide. It was then that I found my calling. I proceeded down the road of elementary education and started striving to set my life plans in order.

At eighteen years of age, I began college. I was determined to get my degree, a job, followed by marriage, then have children and enjoy summers off for family vacations. Well, I did end up with a fun job teaching first grade. I truly loved it, but I was still missing several parts of *my plan*—husband, children, and family vacations!

Fortunately, while in college, I had the privilege of being discipled! Through that experience, I realized that single or married, God had called me to invest my life in others. So, I began striving to do that anytime I felt God had opened a door. I went on many youth trips as a counselor, spent summers working for

BREAKAWAY Ministries, mentored girls at the Big Oak Girls Ranch, and found complete joy in living out 2 Timothy 2:2. I absolutely loved being able to teach and disciple others what God had so graciously taught me through those who had discipled me.

Unfortunately, I was still lonely for my life mate. I remember praying and crying many nights and telling God, despite the loneliness, "I choose You!" I remember watching friend after friend get married and have children. The loneliness some days seemed unbearable. And yet, it pushed me to the feet of Jesus and made me cling to His Word for hope and security. I learned I had to be intentional in my walk with the Lord, and so I sought to strive to do whatever I could not to fall prey to the ways of the world.

As time went on, God truly proved His faithfulness in my life. I laugh at the fact that I can quote nearly all the verses in the Bible on "waiting." I will tell you now that without a doubt, God's timing is Worth the Wait!

I met the most amazing man at thirty-six years of age and married him one month before my thirty-eighth birthday. Now, at the age of forty-two, I am a mother to the cutest, most adorable little boy ever, and I can confidently say that God's timing is perfect! He is trustworthy, faithful, and HE KNOWS THE PLANS HE HAS FOR YOU!

—Leslie Hollowell

Fun Girl Times

1. Flannel Night—Rent a girl flick and have friends over; everyone comes in their flannels. Pop popcorn and have a variety of candy on hand.

2. Bake Night—Girls come with their favorite recipe, including the ingredients. Spend the night in the kitchen baking, then divide goods to go home with each girl who participated.

3. Get a group of friends together and go caroling, then back to your apartment for hot chocolate.

4. You and several friends can adopt a family for Christmas. Take a Saturday before Christmas, meet for breakfast, and then shop together. Go back to your place, wrap all the gifts and then deliver them.

5. Go white water rafting with a group of friends.

6. Start a prayer group with some friends who are as desiring as you are for God to bring you the right mate. Meet once a month to pray.

7. Mocha Latte Night—Have friends over for a variety of coffee drinks. Everyone brings a different flavoring for the coffee.

8. Go for a picnic at the park with friends. Have a Frisbee throwing contest, giving ribbons or prizes for the furthest throw, the shortest throw, the fanciest throw, the most unique throw, the most pitiful throw, etc.

9. Have a Pinterest party. Each guest brings an idea and the supplies to make a craft found on Pinterest. Have one or two recipes prepared to serve that you found on Pinterest.

10. Go with a group of friends to a play and out for dessert. Try a buggy or horse-drawn carriage ride downtown.

11. Need a room in your apartment painted? Have a painting party. If you feed them, they will paint for you! Have a contest as to who can come with the most creative painting attire.

12. Make memories by taking your nieces or nephews out to breakfast every once in a while; they will love it!

13. Have a watermelon carving contest at a picnic with friends. Give prizes for the funniest, the most creative, etc.

14. Start a recreational volleyball team with friends. Many public parks have outdoor volleyball courts.

15. Have a Girls' Spa Day and ask several of your friends to go with you to get a manicure and pedicure, then out to lunch. Or if money is tight, give manicures and pedicures to one another.

16. Journal your way through high school, college, and beyond. You will be amazed years later as you read back through your journals all that God taught you during that time.

17. Take a bike ride through a local park with friends.

18. Try a new restaurant with a friend in a remote part of town where you have never been.

19. Take a day trip with friends to a city—within three to four hours—for shopping, sightseeing, or trying out a new restaurant.

20. Commit one day a month to do a good deed for someone else.

Week 10

Holiday Ideas:
Creative Holiday Decorating and Gift Giving.

Week Ten: A Thanksgiving and Christmas to Remember
Creative Holiday Decorating and Gift Giving

This session is designed to provide the young women with ideas for decorating and gift giving on a limited budget. The Christmas season comes with a great deal of stress, and much of the stress is a result of the expenses that occur. In an effort to help the young women create their own gifts and décor for the holidays, women known for their creativity are invited to demonstrate some fun and creative ways in which the young women can make their own gifts and Christmas decorations. Hands-on instruction is given, showing how fresh greenery can be used to make wreaths and swags for doors or used in table arrangements. Ideas are given for making Christmas ornaments, tree decorations, birthday parties for Jesus, how to share the gospel at Christmas, as well as, the creation of meaningful gifts to be given to family and friends. They are encouraged to bring a friend along to class this week. Leadership will provide a prepared dish or baked good—one of their favorite Christmas recipes to be enjoyed by the class and guests. Hostess will provide coffee and beverage.

If you have more than one Secrets Savored class in your church, you may want to offer this in the evening and combine classes, meeting at the church or in a large home.

Thanksgiving Treasures

"Give thanks with a grateful heart; give thanks to the Holy One. Give thanks because He's given Jesus Christ, God's Son. And now, let the weak say, 'I am strong,' let the poor say, 'I am rich, because of what the Lord has done for us,' Give thanks, give thanks." (Song by Marantha! Music)

Family Blessings and Family Fun

Take time as a family to reflect on God's blessings from the past year. A *Basket Full of Blessings* is a wonderful way for your family to recount, not only God's blessings, but the blessings of each family member. A very small wicker basket is placed at each family member's place setting and at the place of each guest. A large basket in the center of the table contains small strips of paper and pens. On Thanksgiving Day, prior to the meal, each family member and guest uses the strips of paper to write a blessing or Thanksgiving remembrance to each person, placing it in the respective baskets. After the prayer is said, before the meal is served, each person reads their little basket full of blessings. It is a vivid illustration of how we need to encourage and bless one another.

"Oh give thanks to the Lord, for He is good! For His mercy endures forever."
1 Chronicles 16:34, NKJV[10]

---

[21] Maranatha, *Praise 10: O Lord, My Lord.*
[22] Charles Stanley, *The Charles F. Stanley Life Principles Bible: New King James Version* (Thomas Nelson Publishing, 2005).

"In everything give thanks; for this is the will of God in Christ Jesus for you."
1 Thessalonians 5:18, NKJV[22]

Wreath

Begin with a florist foam ring and soak overnight in water. Stand it in the sink to drain thoroughly; flowers will stay fresher longer. To make a sunflower wreath, run florist wire through the back of three sunflower seed heads, and attach in a triangular pattern. Push the flower stems—cut to three to four inches below the bloom—into the foam, filling out the arrangement. Place on front door for a fall welcome to guests. Wreaths can also be used as a centerpiece with a chunky candle in the center.

Indian Corn Garland

Construct an easy-to-assemble Indian corn garland beginning with sisal rope. Dye it a dark brown or a golden maze color. Wrap it with broomcorn, corn tassels (found at farmers' markets), or other dried grasses. Place corn along the rope in a single row or gathered in bunches of three. Wire corn securely in place, and then tie raffia on top for a festive finishing touch. Hang garland from your front door or across your mantel.

Keeping Christ in Christmas

"For unto us a child is born, unto us a Son is given; and the government will be upon His shoulder. And His name will be called Wonderful, Counselor, Mighty God, Everlasting Father, Prince of Peace."
Isaiah 9:6, NKJV[11]

Family Memories

The evening you put up your tree, talk about Christmas and why we celebrate. When placing the nativity, be sure to put it in a prominent place, not under the tree where it will be buried amidst packages. Put it in a place where it will be a constant reminder to your family of the reason we celebrate Christmas—Christ's birth!

In November, let the children make a red-and-green chain with twenty-five loops representing the twenty-five days leading up to Christmas. Number each loop and place a verse related to Christmas on each. Each morning leading up to Christmas, have the children remove one loop and read the verse aloud as a family. You might want to reference the verses from the Christmas story from Matthew 1 and 2, dividing the story among the twenty-five loops.

Make a JOY box for your family. Wrap a box in gold paper with a red-and-green bow. Put small sheets of paper and a pen beside the box under your tree. Family members can write answers to prayers, blessings, and things or names of people that have brought JOY to their lives this past year. On Christmas Day, open the box and share what was written. It will bless your family and bring JOY to your Christmas.

On Christmas Eve, make hot chocolate and serve a birthday cake for Jesus. Have Dad or Granddad read the Christmas story.

On Christmas Eve Day, get the children involved in making costumes to act out the Christmas story that evening. Be creative and use items found around the house. Have the children act out the parts as Dad or Granddad reads the Christmas story.

The wise men came bearing three gifts. To remove the focus from material things, and to keep from overspending, try this with your children this year. Give them each three gifts: one practical (clothing), one spiritual (Bible), and one fun (bike).

---

[23] Charles Stanley, *The Charles F. Stanley Life Principles Bible: New King James Version* (Thomas Nelson Publishing, 2005).

Christmas Creations

Wreaths

- Begin with a grapevine wreath. Gather fresh greenery from your yard or a neighbor's yard; cedar is fragrant and is a wonderful look for this wreath. Starting at one point on the wreath, push cut boughs through the grapevine wreath. Continue placing boughs until complete. Use clippers to trim and shape. Add berries and pinecones, and hang on the front door. Materials needed: grapevine wreath, eastern red cedar boughs, eastern red cedar berries, pinecones, smooth sumac berries, wire as needed, and pruning shears. Tip: Cut the boughs and soak them in water overnight. The next day, let them dry and then begin building your wreath. The extra hydration extends the life of the wreath.

- Begin with a grapevine wreath. Insert clusters of nandina berries to cover wreath. Use strips of florist wire to hold them in place; the berries will hang a little loose due to the nature of the nandina plant. Once berries are in place, use pruners to shape and, using wire, attach other items, such as kumquats, lemons, pears, rose hips, or calamondin oranges—stems still attached. If fruit is without stems, use florist picks. Materials needed: grapevine wreath, nandina berries, calamondin oranges, Meyer lemons, kumquats, rose hips, florist wire, florist picks, and hand pruners.

Tomato Cage Topiaries

Materials needed: garden urn, twelve to fifteen tomato cages for each topiary, duct tape, evergreen garland (fresh or nice fake), cuttings of greenery (such as pine, fir, balsam, and cedar), mini tree lights, wide ribbon, dried pomegranates, and artichokes. These cages retain their original finish, but you can spray paint them a color such as black, silver, gold, copper, or dark green.

- Step One: Invert the cages and join the tips of the wire using a thin strip of duct tape. Stack cages in a garden urn.

- Step Two: Cut a ten-foot piece of evergreen garland. Wire it to the top of the stack of tomato cages, and wrap it around the stacked cages several times. Use florist wire to hold garland in place.

- Step Three: Wire different kinds of greenery into garland for added fullness. Cover top edge of urn with additional greenery all the way to the bottom. Cut wide ribbon into fifteen-inch lengths, and insert it into greenery. Twist a twelve-inch piece of florist wire around the base of each pomegranate and artichoke, and then wire them at intervals to the greenery.

Christmas Candlelight

A single flame flickering in the night creates warmth and an intimate setting; a cluster of candles creates a collective array of sparkle. Ideas such as a tiered fireplace insert can create the warmest of settings for the holiday when lit candles are resting on each arm and the insert is set on a sideboard, at the front door, or within the fireplace itself. Fresh greenery and berries can be placed around the base of the fireplace insert for color and interest. Below are some ideas for creating warmth using candlelight this Christmas season.

- Do you want to find a use for those small sections of leftover gift wrap? Using small glass votives, take the leftover snippets of gift wrap paper and cover the outside of the votives. Cut the paper the width and length of the votive and secure paper edges with double-sticky tape. Tie coordinating ribbon around the votives. Fill with a mix of candles, candies, flowers, or greenery.

- A plant stand can double as a tall candelabrum. Fill small glass fishbowls or jars with cranberries and votive candles (or half can be filled with cranberries and red flowers to add more color). Place one bowl on each arm of the plant stand. Around outer base of the bowl, place sprigs of fresh greenery. Drape red ribbons down the inside pole of the plant stand. This creates a beautiful, warm welcome for guests when placed at the front entrance of your home.

- Line a porch railing, outdoor staircase, walkway, or mantle with clear mason jars or utility lamp covers. Tea lights placed inside make the glass sparkle and create a warm welcome. Fresh greenery and berries at the base add color and interest.

Gift Ideas

- Decorative cellophane bags neatly hold one or two paperwhite bulbs. Nestle the bulb in moist moss sheets, which will provide protection for the bulb and a saucer of moisture. Tie the bag with red decorative ribbon.

- Place a food item in a decorative jar and attach recipe to top along with a festive ribbon. Below is a caramel recipe that is great to give to neighbors, family, and friends.

Creamy Caramel Sauce

1 cup whipping cream
1½ cup firmly packed light brown sugar
1 teaspoon vanilla

½ cup water
¼ cup butter

Bring whipping cream to a simmer in a large saucepan over medium heat, stirring occasionally. Remove from heat and cool. Bring brown sugar and water to a simmer over medium heat, stirring occasionally. Cover and increase heat to medium-high; cook two minutes. Uncover and cook, stirring occasionally, about five minutes or until mixture is golden brown. Remove from heat. Stir in cream mixture, butter, and vanilla. Cool. Store in an airtight container in refrigerator.

Week 10: Optional Review Week

This week is, as it says, optional! If the semester seemed rushed and several key subjects were not taught, the leadership may wish to add this week in order to sufficiently cover the topics missed.

I. Devotional

- Use this week to do a review of this semester's Women of the Bible. Discuss with the young women in class what they learned and were able to apply to their lives from the women studied.

- Pull out questions given in each week's lesson or refer to the question page in the Student Notebook.

II. Lesson

- Looking back over the past lessons, pull out topics that were overlooked due to time restraints and use this week to teach these topics.

- Ask the young women if there was anything in particular that they wished had been taught in the previous weeks and teach it this week.

- Use this week to reemphasize subjects/topics that were rushed in a prior week's lesson due to time restraints.

- Leadership may choose a few of their favorite holiday baking recipes and have a day of fun baking in the kitchen. Or they may want to have the first hour of instruction/teaching on a topic not covered this semester and the second hour set aside to make Christmas sugar cookies—iced and decorated—or one of their own recipes. For a sugar cookie recipe, see Week Six—*Kelly's Very Favorite Sugar Cookie*.

Leader Guide Reference List

A Collection of Favorite Recipes by Cherry House Furniture Galleries. Kearney, NE: Morris Press. 2001.

American Heart Association, "How to Read a Nutrition Label." www.heart.org/HEARTORG/Getting Healthy/NutritionCenter/Nutrition-Center UCM 001188 SubHomePage.jsp

Bellican, Dr. Bill. "The Family Meal for the Holidays . . . Or Every Day? *Mid-South Families,* November 2010.

Goldman, Marcy. *A Passion for Baking.* Birmingham: Oxmoor House Publishing, 2007.

Higgs, Liz Curtis. *Bad Girls of the Bible and What We Learn from Them.* Colorado Springs: Waterbrook Press, 2000.

Katz, David. *The Way to Eat.* Naperville, IL: Sourcebooks, Inc., 2002.

Lewis, Robert. *The New Eve.* Nashville: B&H Publishing Group, 2008.

Marantha! Music. "Give Thanks," 1988. *Praise 10: O Lord, My Lord.*

May, Iva. *W3: Woman, Worldview and the Word.* Chronological Bible Discipleship, 2007. Revised 2010.

Peel, Kathy. "Is Your Kitchen User Friendly?" *HomeLife,* March 2011.

Secrets from the Southern Living Test Kitchens. Birmingham: Oxmoor House Inc., 2002.

Stanley, Charles. *The Charles F. Stanley Life Principles Bible: New King James Version.* Nashville: Thomas Nelson Publishing, 2005.

The Taste of Home Cookbook. Reiman Media Group Inc. 2009.

USDA, "Fact Sheets, Safe Food Handling, Freezing and Food Safety." www.fsis.usda.gov/FactSheets/Focus On Freezing/index.asp

~About the Author~

Dianne Dougharty has been married to her high school sweetheart for over forty years. She is the mother of two daughters and Mimi to seven grandchildren. Dianne graduated from Trevecca Nazarene University with a degree in Elementary Education. For twenty years, she has led women's Bible studies, spoken at conferences, authored curriculum and contributed written work to the *Missional Motherhood* and *My Corner Chair* blog. She has faithfully served beside her husband in full-time vocational ministry.

Dianne has a desire to see older women fulfill the mandate given them in Titus 2:3-4, "These older women must train the younger women to love their husbands and their children, to live wisely and be pure, to work in their homes, to do good, and to be submissive to their husbands. Then they will not bring shame to the word of God." Her heart is for young women to become seekers of Christ, students of God's Word, and lovers of their home, husband, family and calling. She has a passion to see women live purposefully--making investments in the lives of other women.

God led Dianne to develop the *Secrets Savored* eternal *Ministry*, a fun hands-on approach to homemaking which meets in small groups and applies Biblical principles for living a godly life in an often God-less world.

Check out the ministry at www.secretssavored.org.

Follow her on Facebook, Twitter, and Pinterest

Made in the USA
San Bernardino, CA
31 May 2016